rh
25.99

PENELOPE LIVELY

Oleander, Jacaranda

A CHILDHOOD PERCEIVED

VIKING

VIKING

Published by the Penguin Group
Penguin Books Ltd, 27 Wrights Lane, London w8 5tz, England
Penguin Books USA Inc., 375 Hudson Street, New York, New York 10014, USA
Penguin Books Australia Ltd, Ringwood, Victoria, Australia
Penguin Books Canada Ltd, 10 Alcorn Avenue, Toronto, Ontario, Canada m4v 3b2
Penguin Books (NZ) Ltd, 182–190 Wairau Road, Auckland 10, New Zealand

Penguin Books Ltd, Registered Offices: Harmondsworth, Middlesex, England

First published 1994
1 3 5 7 9 10 8 6 4 2
First edition

All photographs are the author's own

Filmset in 12/15.5 pt Monotype Garamond
Typeset by Datix International Limited, Bungay, Suffolk
Printed in England by Clays Ltd, St Ives plc

A CIP catalogue record for this book is available from the British Library

isbn 0–670–85470–0

for my children, and for theirs

Preface

This is a book about childhood. It is also a discussion of the nature of childhood perception and a view of Egypt in the 1930s and 1940s. My childhood is no more – or less – interesting than anyone else's. It has two particularities. One is that I was the product of one society but was learning how to perceive the world in the ambience of a quite different culture. I grew up English, in Egypt. The other is that I was cared for by someone who was not my mother, and that it was a childhood which came to an abrupt and traumatic end. In 1945, when I was twelve, my parents were divorced and I was taken to England, and to boarding school. It was to be a grim rite of passage.

I have tried to recover something of the anarchic vision of childhood – in so far as any of us can do such a thing – and use this as the vehicle for a reflection on the way in which children perceive. I believe that the experience of childhood is irretrievable. All that remains, for any of us, is a headful of brilliant frozen moments, already dangerously distorted by the wisdoms of maturity. But it has seemed to me that it might be possible to take these pictures in the mind – those moments of seeing – and, by turning them into language, to try both to look at the way in which a child sees and at how this matches up with what it was that was seen. And since what was being seen requires explanation and discussion also, I have written of Egypt, and of Palestine and the Sudan – of the reality as well as of my childcentred perception.

Which raises the question of the nature of reality itself. Definitions of reality depend on who is doing the defining, of course. My view of reality today is very different from the one I held when I was four, or six, or eight – views which were equally valid at the time and in many ways rather more interesting. My adult view of reality is conditioned like anyone else's by culture and education. The childhood view – like that of any other child – is anarchic, because without preconceptions. When you do not know what to expect of the world – when everything is astonishing – then anything is possible and acceptable. Children are aliens in a landscape that is entirely unpredictable, required to conform to the dictation of a mysterious code while finding their way around a world which is both dazzling and perverse. I wanted to see if it was possible to uncover something of this experience.

While I was thinking about the writing of this book, and jotting down notes, I had a dream one night which by the light of day seemed so heftily symbolic as to be a parody of the form, so I write it down, though I'm not sure that I would care to try to unravel the various elements of the symbolism. I was in a large barn filled with a mixture of straw, hay and earth – a compacted mass which I felt compelled to excavate. I seemed to be trying to tidy it up in some way. As I dug down I came to a layer which made me uneasy – there were bits of cardboard and plastic and I suspected that something was concealed, something disagreeable. I came upon the handles of a child's pushchair or buggy, and as I began to pull it out I saw that there was a thing – a figure – sitting in it. A dressed figure – I saw shoes and a sunbonnet. I thought with gathering dismay that this might be a dead child, and I pulled the whole object out and took it to a lighter place where I could inspect it. I didn't want to do this, but knew that I was somehow bound to. I considered fetching someone to help me, but knew also that I had to do this alone. I put my hand on the sunbonnet and felt something round which I feared was the child's skull. Then I pulled the bonnet off, and saw that there was simply a doll – a china doll. I had a feeling of immense relief, and went outside the barn where I found a group of people which included my son, and told them what had happened. They shared my relief.

There it is – raw stuff. Not something I would be capable of inventing, either. And there also is the surreal vision which shares something, it seems to me, with the vision of childhood. The willingness to suspend disbelief. Perhaps there is an eerie affinity between the strange offerings of the subconscious and the unfettered view of the child. It struck me as appropriate that a book which tried to pin down the latter should be heralded by a particularly lurid instance of the former.

Chapter One

We are going by car from Bulaq Dakhrur to Heliopolis. I am in the back. The leather of the seat sticks to my bare legs. We travel along a road lined at either side with oleander and jacaranda trees, alternate splashes of white and blue. I chant, quietly: 'Jacaranda, oleander . . . Jacaranda, oleander . . .' And as I do so there comes to me the revelation that in a few hours' time we shall return by the same route and that I shall pass the same trees, in reverse order – oleander, jacaranda, oleander, jacaranda – and that, by the same token, I can look back upon myself of now, of this moment. I shall be able to think about myself now, thinking this – but it will be then, not now.

And in due course I did so, and perceived with excitement the chasm between past and future, the perpetual slide of the present. As, writing this, I think with equal wonder of that irretrievable child, and of the eerie relationship between her mind and mine. She is myself, but a self which is unreachable except by means of such miraculously surviving moments of being: the alien within.

*

Here is a child thinking about time, experiencing a sudden illumination about chronology and a person's capacity for recollection. In terms of developmental psychology, this would be seen as significant, an indication of a particular achievement – the ability to be actively concerned with the general nature of things. But the findings and the discussion of developmental psychology can make oddly frustrating reading – they reflect the process of scientific observation and are hence illuminating, but they seem to have no apparent bearing on the rainbow experience we have all lost, but of which we occasionally retrieve a brilliant glimpse. I know now what was going on in my head that day over fifty years ago. I can turn the cold eye of adult knowledge and experience upon the moment and interpret it in the light of a lifetime's reading and reflection. But what seems most astonishing of all is that something of the reality of the moment survives this destructive freight of wisdom and rationality, firmly hitched to the physical world. In my mind, there is still the tacky sensation of the leather car-seat which sticks to the back of my knees. I see still the bright flower-laden trees. I roll the lavish names around on the tongue: 'Jacaranda, oleander . . .' For this is an incident infused with the sense of language quite as much as with a perception of the nature of time: the possession and control of these decorative words, the satisfaction of being able to say them, display them. Though all of it was done, I know, in privacy: this interesting perception, the significance of it and the excitement, had to be mine alone, uncommunicated. And now, appropriately, the adult with whom I share it is myself.

We would have been going to visit friends, driving from our home four miles west of the centre of Cairo to Heliopolis, the eastern suburb, a journey which meant traversing the city – a slow and incident-strewn navigation amid trams and donkey-carts and pedestrians. Cairo was traffic-ridden, as now, but it was a less daunting traffic than the ceaseless roar of today. The population of Cairo was then just over 1 million, as compared with the 14 million of today. Bulaq Dakhrur, where we lived, was a mud village in open fields, with, just beyond it, three substantial European-owned houses surrounded by large gardens, one of which was ours.

Bulaq el Dakhrur, correctly. We curtailed the name, using it to mean both the place and our own home. And it was in its correct form that it leaped at me from road signs almost forty years later, on my first return to Egypt. It was not a place now, but an area, a part of Cairo's sprawling extension. The city's teeming dun-coloured spread had gobbled up the fields of *berseem* and sugar-cane, the villages, and presumably our home. I was prepared for this, and thought it unlikely that it could still exist. But I had come there partly to look for it.

It was my first return to Egypt. Over the years it had somehow never been possible – either too expensive, or impracticable. But the 1980s brought the expansion of the Egyptian tourist industry and the benefaction of relatively cheap tours, and thus it was that I went back as a tourist, packaged up the Nile along with Jack, my husband, and our friends Ann and Anthony Thwaite. We had three days in Cairo, during which we had planned the search for Bulaq Dakhrur. I did not know how to find it, except that you went west out of Cairo, over a railway line by way of a level crossing, and then on a bit and it was to the left. The population of the Bulaq el Dakhrur area was now around a quarter of a million, we had been told.

I had an introduction to an Arabic-speaking Cairo resident, Cordelia Salter, who gamely agreed to come with us as translator. We set off from the Ramses Hilton in a taxi, whose driver accepted with enthusiasm the proposal of this eccentric quest. A few hours before, in the hotel room, I had dialled the phone number that has been in my head all my life: 96245. A discontinued line. Of course.

We reached the railway line. The level crossing was automated now. Was this the place at which we used to sit in the car, waiting for the anticipated arrival and eventual interminable passage of a goods train? We would be there for half an hour, sometimes, slotted into a long impatient line of carts and trucks, with those who could hooting continuously, others bawling at the signalmen, and anyone on foot climbing over the barrier and crawling under the train, which was frequently stationary. I studied the new, efficient-looking arrangement and suddenly it came to me that just beyond the railway

4

line there should be a canal, and indeed there was. But now the road curved off to the right in a way that seemed to me wrong. There was a sea of shabbily built apartment blocks on all sides, balconies festooned with washing, the street strewn with rubble, people everywhere, children running around like puppies, more of the same visible down every alley. I began to feel like a time traveller, seeing still the white-dappled clover fields and the waving sugar-cane.

Definitely, the road was going too far to the right. We stopped the taxi and the driver did some astute thinking and vanished into a coffee-house to see if he could find some old men who would remember this area way back and who might know if there were still any large old houses surviving. He returned, triumphant. Yes, someone had said there were houses that used to belong to English people, but not on this road, which was built in 1970. Over to the left. Down that way . . . Vague gesturing.

We set off again, plunging now down pot-holed side roads, the taxi moving amid the rubble at a walking pace. We began to acquire an interested following. Passers-by interrogated the taxi driver. The news of our mission spread and the following increased. We acquired a man wearing a suit and carrying a briefcase – an incongruous figure in these parts – who offered to act as escort. We were now seven in the taxi. At every street junction – if such they could be called – the driver stopped once more. Consultations were held. People pointed, in various directions. Others shook their heads dismissively. We were all by now hot and tired.

And then someone said very positively: 'Down there . . .' The street indicated was wider than most, but so ferociously pot-holed that it seemed wise to take to our feet. We walked a hundred yards or so, escorted by our entourage which had swollen to twenty or thirty. And there suddenly was a large, very dilapidated house which certainly had a whiff of familiarity. A pillared porch, green shutters . . . But it didn't seem right. I studied it. Everyone else watched me, expectantly. 'No,' I said unhappily, 'I don't think it is.'

We continued. Beyond the building was a newish mosque surrounded by tenements. And then a bit of waste ground and then . . . There it was. Bulaq Dakhrur. Standing there battered but alive, the old shutters still on most of the windows, the big veranda at the back, the front porch, the whole infinitely familiar outline that has featured in my dreams for forty years. I said, 'This is it.'

Beaming smiles all round. My companions emotional. The entourage congratulating each other, and me. The first house we came to, I now realized, had been that of our then neighbours. The middle house of the three had been replaced by the mosque and Bulaq Dakhrur stood isolated, fenced off behind railings with a gate at which appeared a *gaffir*, who opened up at once with broad smiles when all was explained. The house was now the administrative offices of a technical school, apparently –

and there in what had once been our garden were the concrete block-houses which were the workshops and classrooms. But it was the lunch hour and there was no one around. We trooped into the precincts, all fifty of us, and I led a sort of royal progress round the outside of the house, taking photographs, while founder members of our entourage explained to latecomers what it was all about. The man with the briefcase presided benignly, as if it had all been his doing. Everyone shook hands with everyone else. It was not possible to go inside because it was locked up. I didn't really want to anyway. This was quite enough. The *gaffir* had been associated with the place for long enough to know something of its past. He launched on an explanation to our companion interpreter, pointing to an open space filled with rubbish, cats and playing children – and as he pointed I saw a rectangle of razed concrete walling, with a shallow square pit alongside it, like archaeological remains. The fragments of our swimming-pool and the engine-house in which lived our electricity generator.

Of the surroundings, everything had gone. The fields, the village, the palm-fringed canals. Our garden, with its thirty-foot eucalyptus trees, the lawns, the ponds, the pergolas. Nothing left but the house, stolidly clinging on. Somehow, this was not sad but curiously exhilarating. I had not expected it to be there at all. And now the building seemed in some odd way to have the dignity of the Sphinx, which looks aloofly out over the degradation all around. Bulaq Dakhrur did not seem aloof – quite comfortable indeed, rather like a person who has settled to changed circumstances but does not abandon identity. And to be the only person to have known it both then and now gave me a strange sensation of complicity with a physical object – as though it had the intimacy of life.

There were more complex reactions, too. I felt as though a piece of myself were there, and that I had come back to fetch it. A wave of happiness; a sense of completion. And there was also the powerful feeling that on some other plane of existence the Ur-house was still there also, with the eucalyptus avenue and the lawns and the flower beds, and I with it, a ghost-child for ever riding my bike up and down the drive, or trailing around after the gardeners, or reading in my vine hammock in the hedge hideaway.

And there was also a response to this dramatic metamorphosis which was more detached – a perception of the battered house as an expression of a world that was utterly extinguished – the Egypt of foreign administration and also an England of assumptions that are now unthinkable. Half of me was preoccupied with a contorted nostalgia; the other half was asking questions about the landscape of resurrection all around, the rubble and the concrete-mixers. How does Cairo sustain such a population? What do people do? How do the *fellaheen* live today?

I don't know how old I was on the day of the drive to Heliopolis. Probably six or seven. I was born in Cairo, and when I was two we moved from the flat in Zamalek to Bulaq Dakhrur – my parents, myself and Lucy, who had looked after me since I was six months old. I was an only child, and as I grew Lucy was the centre of my existence, my surrogate mother. My parents were peripheral figures of whom I did not see a great deal, for whom I felt an interested regard but no intense commitment. The continuous points of reference through all these glimmering fragments of that time are a person and a place – Lucy's firm presence, and the equally indestructible backcloth – the sharp precision of the house and the garden with beyond them the fields and the canals, the people, the animals, the feathery palms, the tall rustling sugar-cane, and, further yet, the maelstrom of Cairo, with its trams and gharries and gridlocked lines of donkey-carts, the minarets against the blue sky and the wide brown river. I had known nowhere else; it was absolutely familiar and absolutely reassuring.

I am walking with Lucy beside the canal. This is one of our regular afternoon walks, a favourite with me because halfway along the canal there is a mimosa tree, from which Lucy allows me to pick a sprig. I bury my nose in the powdery yellow balls, guzzling that strange, fragile smell. Further along there is a place where children from the village bathe in the canal, stark naked, hurling themselves from an overhanging branch, throwing up great plumes of foaming brown water. And there am I in my cotton dress, my sun-hat, my lace-up shoes and my socks: I stare at them with fascination and with envy. Further yet, though, there is a potential hazard.

Sometimes there is a gamoose – a water buffalo – tethered under a particular tree. I am scared of gamooses: they are enormous and they glare at you with sunken eyes, swinging their heads from side to side. Moreover, they are said to be maddened by the smell of Europeans. I creep past this gamoose on the far side of the track, heart thumping, trying to be odourless, eyeing its horns and the frayed rope tether.

The expectation of life in rural Egypt then was around forty. Infant mortality was high. My stare of envy was also one of absolute ignorance. The canals, the lifeblood of the agricultural landscape, were also open sewers, used for washing clothes and cooking-utensils, for watering animals, for urinating and defecating, for drinking. They were the habitat of the snails which harboured bilharzia, the deadly debilitating disease of the Egyptian *fellaheen*. Many of those children would have had trachoma, the eye complaint which causes blindness. Only a small proportion of them received primary education.

I knew about poverty. It was visible on all sides – on the gaunt visages of old men, on the fly-ridden faces of babies, in the skinny animals, the rags and tatters, the glimpses through the doors of village hovels. People begged – everywhere, all the time. Conjuring it all up today, I see what I now know – I see the infant mortality figures and the catalogue of disease and the system of economic oppression. Then, I saw simply what I had always seen, with the impervious accepting eye of childhood. This was the world. How could it be otherwise?

It was a landscape that was bright green and grey-green and tawny. The fields of *berseem* were brilliant emerald dappled with white clover flowers, the sugar-cane was grey-green ripening to golden and the palms were grey-green and so were the eucalyptus trees and the casuarinas that lined the canals. The dusty paths that criss-crossed the fields were tawny, as were the village huts. It was also a landscape of perpetual motion – the waving palms and the rippling crops and the endless pilgrimages of animals and of people. It teemed with life – the processions of donkeys so laden with berseem or cane that they were simply four titupping legs topped by a green mound, the long columns of camels, the flocks of goats. Each field was populous – busy with stooping figures, *galabiyas* tucked up between their legs as they worked: men, women, children. When I came to England I was perplexed by the empty Somerset countryside. Where was everybody? And now it is in medieval painting that I find the Egyptian landscape of the 1940s – in Brueghel above all. There it is again – the scene of a peasant society, the agricultural economy of intensive labour.

In the midst of this we walked, Lucy and I, for exercise and for occupation – the only people there who knew the meaning of leisure. Attracting attention – naturally enough. Children trailed after us, clamouring for *baksheesh*. Everyone noted our passage. I do not remember overt hostility – though I cannot see why not, now, knowing what I know. It was the animals I feared – the pi-dogs hurtling from behind a wall, barking blue murder. The dreaded gamooses.

The whole place smelt – of dust and dung. A not unpleasant smell – rich and organic and so deeply familiar that it was intrinsic, an element like the heat and the noise of invisible insects. Camel dung and donkey dung and the dark green liquid pools left by the gamooses which spattered every path. And outside the village huts sat the women and the girls making fuel out of dung and straw, up to their elbows in it, slapping the flat pancakes from hand to hand and piling them up into the great mounds that stood outside every door. They watched us as we passed, patently discussing us. Sometimes there would be a gust of ribald laughter. *'Sa'eeda,'* we said. *'Sa'eeda,'* they replied. *'Sa'eeda, Sa'eeda.'* *'Baksheesh,'* clamoured the children. The babies crawled in the dust, their faces black with flies.

Our European enclave of the three substantial, garden-encircled houses sat in the landscape like some incongruous island, lapped on all sides by 'the cultivation', as we called it. The daily walks with Lucy are merged now into one single acute recollection, in which the whole thing hangs suspended in vibrant detail – the mimosa and the naked leaping children and the grey mud-caked threatening spectres of the gamooses. The pink and blue and lime green of children's clothes, the white of *galabiyas*, the black humps of squatting women.

The soft flop of a camel's foot on the dusty path; the felt-shod tapping of a donkey. All of it was both mundane and arresting. I saw it, received it, and did not query.

One occasion only projects from this bland acceptance. We were visited by a relative who was in the colonial service, a District Commissioner from the Sudan. Bored stiff by the polite social whirl laid on by my mother, I suspect, he headed one day for the cultivation. Eluding Lucy, I trailed after him, fascinated by this forthright, knowledgeable figure. To my surprise and alarm he made straight for the village, instead of the picturesque canal walk. Surely we were not going there? One skirted villages, normally: the smells, the pi-dogs, the droves of begging children. But my relative strode into the very centre of the place, scattering dogs with a few well-aimed stones, patting the heads of children, throwing out greetings in all directions, volleys of Arabic which brought the women to their doors and the men from the coffee-house. Within minutes we were ushered towards someone's mud hut. I was by now silent with amazement. Could we be going inside? Such was my indoctrination about dirt and disease that I assumed I should drop dead instantly. Entranced and horrified I edged gingerly behind him into the hot gloom of the interior and tried to squat like everyone else, keeping warily in the lee of my by now awesome relative. He was already firing questions at the family, in the firm tradition of benevolent paternalism. How many children? How many wives? Cattle, goats? How much land? What crops? Current price of sugar-cane? He yanked a small child towards him, tutted over an infected eye, rapped out instructions. A platter of unleavened bread was produced and offered – those flat loaves cooked on open ovens in the village street. My relative helped himself to a chunk and sat absently chewing while he continued to shoot questions and receive the lengthy replies. I gazed intently: he would keel over now, for sure, dead as they come. But no, he continued to squat there in rude health, knees jutting up from his khaki shorts, making jokes, if you please. Our host was doubled up with laughter, the women clutched black veils to their mouths, convulsed with genteel mirth. Only the children shared my appalled fascination at this unprecedented scene. They clustered in a corner, infants occasionally crawling out from the huddle to be batted back by an adult hand. We eyed each other, poles apart but eerily attuned.

There is a touch of embellishment here, I have to admit. I cannot have known what it was he said to those people – I did not understand Arabic well enough. The land and the crops and the price of sugar-cane I supply with the wisdoms of today, but the general tenor of it all was clear enough to me back then, along with the eccentricity of the whole occasion and the unsettling observation that it was eccentric to me but not at all so to him, which threw a disturbing light on my assumptions.

I think that by then I was about nine. I find the episode intriguing because I can recover my own feelings of bewilderment and disorientation, and because I can now see objectively that it seems to be an instance of a child becoming aware of the existence of other viewpoints – an erosion of the egocentric vision of childhood. And the whole thing is complicated by the further dimension of cultural assumptions. I saw that peasant family with a new clarity, both stepping aside from my own customary viewpoint and shedding for an instant the obscuring wisdoms of the adults I knew: Lucy, my parents, their friends. I saw that there is more than one way of looking at the world, and was startled.

The analysis and discussion of childhood development is disappointingly deficient when it comes to an examination of the way in which children cope with the intricacies of social and cultural life. I can see why. It is hard if not impossible to quantify in accordance with scientific method. You can set up experiments and ask questions and analyse the answers but somewhere along the way you have lost entirely the mercurial quality of the actual process – the extraordinary way in which children learn to negotiate the jungle in which they find themselves, and the parallel achievement whereby they discover that theirs is not the only negotiation – that experience is universal, and that it is expedient to discover how others experience. The investigation of the nature of children's egocentric vision centres on their conquest of the physical world – the way in which babies learn that an object or a person continues to exist when out of sight, the way in which small children are – or are not – able to conceive of a different viewpoint in the most basic sense. If you ask a child to position a model figure behind a model wall so that it could not be seen by a putative person on the opposite side of the table, can it do so? The answer seems to be – yes, rather better than has been previously believed. The stern Piagetian credo of the unfaltering egocentric vision has been considerably modified. Small children are more flexible than we thought.

But what interests me most is what happens around and beyond this basic diagnosis of perception. How do children arrive at an alternative interpretation of things, and what happens to them on the way? And this is where developmental psychology begins to give up, it seems to me – for good reason. But we all go through this process of discovery – unless dangerously warped. The answers are there inside the head, if only they could be called up. It is as though there were a raft of submerged material from which there floats up from time to time some perfect fragment – a shining morsel of experience whose brilliance makes all the more tantalizing that unavailable mass. And the shining fragments, you come to realize, are there because, once retrieved, the mind makes sure to keep them untarnished. You take them out and look them over, to keep them in good condition. But down there are many more – apparently unreachable through any deliberate process of retrieval. Just occasionally, something new shakes free and comes gleaming to the surface, and you recognize it, surprised. Of course – that was always there. And yet it wasn't.

Every child has to cope with the confusing codes of its own society – beginning with the family and working outwards. Every child is confronted with the puzzle of class distinctions. My particular challenge was that I was growing up in accordance with the teachings of one culture but surrounded by all the signals of another. Egypt was my home, and all that I knew, but I realized that in some perverse way I was not truly a part of it.

We were English. I was English – that much I knew, deep in my being. It was of central importance – you were never allowed to forget that – but what it meant I could not possibly have said. I had been to England briefly for summer visits, before the outbreak of war made this impossible. I remembered little of it, except a windy Cornish beach and my grandmother's flower-filled garden. More interesting and memorable were the long sea trips there and back – the rusty saltwater baths and the creaking cabins and the ranks of rug-wrapped figures in deck chairs. So far as I was concerned England was a place a long way away which was nothing much to do with me, except that in some mysterious and solemn way it was, and don't you forget it.

I was conditioned partly by my parents and the society in which we lived, but most of all by Lucy. Lucy's patriotism was absolute and implacable. There was English, and there was other. To be English was to be among the chosen and saved; to be other was simply to be other. There were gradations of other. American or Australian was other but within shouting distance, as it were. French, Italian, Greek were becoming unreachable, everything else was outer space. Within this unrelenting xenophobia there was a stern creed of tolerance and respect for alien practices, especially religious practice. I knew that it was offensive to stare when Muslims were at prayer, that mosques must be entered with the same reverence as Cairo's Church of England cathedral. The world of other was different, and hence of no great interest, but you accorded it a perfect right to carry on as it did.

My parents' views are more indistinct, but were certainly a tempered form of Lucy's, and reflected those of the society from which they sprang. Their friends were mainly English, invigorated here and there by an infusion of cosmopolitan Cairo. They were perhaps less single-mindedly patriotic than Lucy, and more overtly curious about Egypt, but then so they should have been – they had the advantage of education and, in my mother's case, of unlimited leisure. Their concerns roved wider, but they too left me in no doubt that we were all of us in some mysterious way hitched up to this distant and inconceivable place of which I knew so little.

England was pink. I knew that from Bartholomew's atlas. Pink was good. And there was plenty of it, too, a global rash; lots of the rest of Africa, and India slung there like a pear, and New Zealand and Australia and Canada and much else. I learned history from a book called *Our Island Story*, much approved by Lucy. It had glossy romantic pictures of national heroes, with potted accounts of the finer moments of the nation's rise to pink glory. Boadicea and King Arthur and Sir Walter Raleigh and Kitchener and Queen Victoria all somehow rolled into one to produce essence of Englishness. The atlas reinforced this triumphant digest of the Whig interpretation of history. Up there at the top is brave little England. Britannia rules the waves. Goodbye Piccadilly, farewell Leicester Square. This sceptred isle. John Bull. The white cliffs of Dover. I imbibed it all with a whisper of unease: did I truly have a claim to all this?

I look back in dismay. There has been a lot of unlearning to do. And can it all be unlearned? Is there perhaps deep within me some unreconstructed layer which believes pink is best and that it has been uphill all the way from brave Boadicea to good Lord Kitchener?

Egypt was not pink but diagonally striped with pink – a worrying ambiguity. If anybody had ever stopped to explain to me why exactly the British were in Egypt, in such numbers and with such authority – why indeed we ourselves were there – the explanation had not sunk in. I saw cosmopolitan, polyglot Cairo. I recognized differences and distinctions – the poverty of the fellaheen, the luxury and flamboyance of shops and cafés, the varying rituals of the place from the muezzin's call to the social exchanges of Gezira Sporting Club or Shepheard's Hotel, and perceived it all as an immutable state of affairs, requiring observation but no explanation. I noted with beady eyes, as any child does. The notes taken are with me still; now, I can interpret them.

Those confusing stripes indicated a Protectorate, of course, and the atlas was out of date anyway because by then the country had been accorded an ambivalent form of independence whereby Britain retained control over defence, foreign policy and security of communications, and foreign nationals remained subject to their own, rather than Egyptian, law. It was not independence at all, as Egyptians were well aware, and throughout the 1930s and 1940s the dispute continued between the nationalist movement and the British government until eventually full independence was achieved in 1952 after the revolution and the departure of King Farouk. But in my childhood the country was still dominated by a foreign superstructure. In 1937 there were 31,000 British in Egypt, as well as 18,000 French, 47,000 Italians and 68,000 Greeks. Along with plentiful communities of Maltese, Lebanese, Syrians and, of course, the Turks who had been running the place in one form or another since Mameluke times. Egypt had a king (the former line of khedives had been indulgently turned into a hereditary monarchy with King Fouad, Farouk's father), a democratically elected government and a prime minister, but it was still effectively run by foreigners, and principally by the British. It was a Muslim society whose population spoke Arabic, whose king was of Turkish descent, and which was superficially European. The architecture of modern Cairo – by which I mean nineteenth-century Cairo, most of it now demolished, more's the pity – was French: the elegant apartment blocks with their balconies and tall shuttered windows, the Haussmann-style boulevards. The shops were likely to be owned and staffed by Greeks, Lebanese or Italians. The public works were constructed and administered by French, Germans, British. Government offices were manned by Egyptians, but behind every Egyptian stood a British official.

It had always been thus, of course. Greek, Roman, Mameluke. A brief and nasty experience of Napoleon. And then a period of tottering bankruptcy under the khedives before the British and French intervened in the late nineteenth century to sort out the economic crisis and, of course, keep a stranglehold over the crucial building and administration of the Suez canal. Egyptians had had two thousand years of foreign occupation, reflected now as then in the emotive wealth of the landscape, in which everything happens at once – Greek temples and Roman forts and the mosques of the Mamelukes and eventually the great cosmopolitan jumble of Cairo. With the unimaginable enigmatic reach of the pharaonic centuries beyond.

We were a part of the tail-end of that occupation. My father had gone out to Cairo as a very young man to work in the National Bank of Egypt. In the final years of the war he was made manager of the bank's Sudan branch, where my mother, Lucy and I joined him briefly in Khartoum for the winter period when it was considered that we could endure the climate. He spent his youth in Egypt, effectively. When I asked him once, in his old age, what his feelings were about the place he replied, quite simply: 'I loved it.'

In my head, my father is hugely tall and pink-faced and forever genial – roaring with laughter in the midst of a party of people on the veranda at Bulaq Dakhrur, or sticking his head round the nursery door to pass the time of day and tease me for a few minutes. In the photos in which I sit on his knee or am carried on his back, he is touchingly young, peering out at me now behind small owlish glasses with his distinctive look, some genetic quirk which preserves him still in my own face, and those of my two half brothers – the sons he achieved years later in another marriage – and which surprised me recently in a sudden glance from my own baby grandson. He bequeathed me the short sight and the long limbs, too, though not perhaps the inextinguishable good humour. In my adolescence, I got to know him, but during my Egyptian childhood he existed only on the perimeters of my vision – getting into the Ford V8 to drive to Cairo and his office, or at the hub of the downstairs adult life with which I was not much concerned, hived off with Lucy in our upstairs domain. And now I realize that he lived partly in another world, of which I knew – and know – little. He spoke good French and some Arabic, and was in the course of his job in daily contact with many people beyond the cloistered circles of Gezira Sporting Club and Shepheard's Hotel. He was a part of the whole convoluted and precarious system of the foreign administration of the country.

And I knew little or nothing of all this, back then. Nothing of why we were there and the implications of our presence, except that some curious process of absorption without comprehension must have gone on, because when I read now of that time, the pages are littered with significance. Hands wave from the text. I know these names: Khedive Ismail, Mohammed Ali, Sa'ad Zaghloul, Nahas Pasha, Sir Miles Lampson. It is as though I have discovered the key to some baffling code. Some of the names, of course, were part of the topography of Cairo: Khedive Ismail Bridge over the Nile, flanked by imperious lions for which I felt wild nostalgia when in my grieving adolescence I first saw the lions in Trafalgar Square. Sharia Mohammed Ali. But the names of Sa'ad Zaghloul, the powerful and popular leader of the Wafd party, and of Nahas Pasha, the subsequent prime minister, must have been constantly mentioned. I heard, and noted. I remember a great fuss about tanks and Abdin Palace and the King and the Ambassador which would have been the notorious occasion in 1942 when Sir Miles Lampson, accompanied by the GOC of troops in Egypt, drove to Abdin Palace with an escort of armoured cars (the tanks seem now to have been apocryphal) to insist that Farouk invite Nahas Pasha to form a government. Something of the drama must have penetrated my tranquil existence, but from my point of view the main interest of the King was his girth, held up to me as a dire warning by Lucy: 'If you eat too many sweets you'll get fat like King Farouk.'

Lucy was one of that army of semi-professional

women to whom, in those days, middle-class English mothers entrusted their children. It now seems to me extraordinary to hand over your child to someone else to be brought up but I cannot, in retrospect, blame my mother. She was merely behaving as everyone she knew did; to have done otherwise would have been an act of defiant unconventionality. As it was, she looked after me on Wednesday afternoons, and in theory she 'had' me for an hour after tea, though this custom was abandoned if inconvenient. My main recollection of my mother is of someone exhaustively involved in 'seeing people' – Cairo's social life was frenetic. In the mind's eye, she is for ever part of a group on a lawn in the glowing light of early evening, everyone tricked out with white cotton mosquito protection tubes on arms and legs so that they looked like Michelin men, ice-clinking glasses of whisky and soda in their hands. Of no interest at all to me; upstairs was Lucy, and my own world. The arrangement was entirely satisfactory, so far as I was concerned.

Now, I see everything that was wrong with it, not least for Lucy herself – a maternal woman condemned like all her kind to be for ever a surrogate mother to other people's children. She was a Londoner, and had started off as nursery maid to aristocratic families, which had instilled in her a reverence for titles which I found hard to handle when I saw her in adult life. Back then, Lucy's particular form of élitism washed over me – a Lord or a Lady had as little resonance for me as a Pasha or a General or a Bishop. Words – no more and no less.

Lucy was indeed the fountain of all knowledge, so far as I was concerned. I was in no doubt that what she spoke was the gospel, but those aspects of it which meant nothing to me I passed over.

I see and hear her now, quite clearly. A small woman – by the time I was eleven I was as tall as she was. Dark hair, long, but worn always in a bun secured with hairpins. To glimpse her in the mornings with her hair loose was to see her oddly – and a touch dismayingly – exposed. The hairpins were endlessly fascinating: I used to steal them. Round, steel-framed spectacles. She always wore grey or navy: grey cotton dresses for daily use, a grey suit or a navy coat for afternoons off or special outings. Stockings, always. A grey or navy felt hat, frequently. Her London speech had been gentrified entirely – when I met her sisters in England after the war I was startled because they spoke differently. She had stern moral values – a general code of truthfulness and honesty and kindness spiced with fervent patriotism. All this rubbed off on to me except the patriotism which was always elusive because of my confusion about my own identity. I could never manage to feel English with quite the confidence that Lucy did.

She was my entire emotional world. I lived alone with her, locked into a reassuring arrangement of solicitude and dependence. My parents were satellite figures – occasionally stimulating or provocative, but of a different order. Peering backwards, I cannot really see them. Lucy is vivid. She seems in retrospect to have been ageless; I know now that she was in her thirties.

We were together all of the time, as a parent and child would be. Except for Wednesdays, when she had her afternoon off and I was left with my mother, an arrangement which I disliked but endured because I recognized that Lucy was entitled to a spree and I could look forward to the blow-by-blow account she would give me of the film she had been to at one of the Cairo cinemas – a Bob Hope or a Hedy Lamarr or a Deanna Durbin. I was uncomfortable with my mother and played her up, I'm sure, sensing her own unease with me. She was not good with children. Lucy, when at odds with her, was fond of recounting caustically to her cronies my mother's pronouncement that it took a particular mentality to be able to look after children – an inferior one, by implication.

I am in bed, on the brink of sleep. I can hear the voices of Lucy and my mother, across the passage, pitched low, in dispute. Lucy's voice is tight and contemptuous; my mother's is shrill and defensive. And it comes to me that it is Lucy who has the whip-hand, which is confusing. Why is there that note in my mother's voice? Why can Lucy say what she does?

My mother needed Lucy very much more than Lucy needed her. Lucy could have found another job a dozen times over within twenty-four hours in war-time Cairo. Had she left, my mother would have been faced with the daunting task of searching for an acceptable substitute, or the unthinkable alternative of looking after me herself.

So Lucy enjoyed absolute autonomy within her own sphere and considerable licence without. She had reservations about my mother; from time to time her disapproval burst out. She stayed, I think, for my sake. And in my presence she would always have adopted a neutral stance. That half-heard exchange was a glimpse of a side to their relationship I was not supposed to know about.

Chapter Two

I am lying on a sofa, knees hugged to my chest, staring at the sofa back, which is a blurry chintz patterned with flowers, large blue and green pansies. I have a pain in my stomach. I trace the petals of the pansies with my finger. The pain comes in great waves, ebbing and flowing, washing through me as though I were in the grip of some tide. Lucy is somewhere in the room, knitting. I can hear the clack of needles. There is just the blurred pansies, and the clicking noise, and the pain.

The mosquito net over my bed is suspended from the ceiling by a metal hoop, and tucked in under the mattress all around. I am inside a filmy white tent. The tent is filled with the metallic smell of Flit. I can see the outline of the Flit-gun on the table beside the bed, a chunky barrel with a pump handle. I can see also the grey smudges of squashed mosquitoes on the net and a long wavering white line where Lucy has mended a tear.

I have found a praying mantis in the hedge. A shaft of sunlight makes it translucent. I can see its insides, and the dark veining of its wings, and the globes of its eyes. It sits in a frozen posture, and then moves an arm, stiffly, like an automaton.

No thought at all here, just observation – the young child's ability to focus entirely on the moment, to direct attention upon the here and now, without the intrusion of reflection or of anticipation. It is also the Wordsworthian vision of the physical world: the splendour in the grass. And, especially, Virginia Woolf's creation of the child's eye view. A way of seeing that is almost lost in adult life. You can stare, you can observe – but within the head there is now the unstoppable obscuring onward rush of things. It is no longer possible simply to see, without the accompanying internal din of meditation.

And is that perhaps why we remember with such clarity? Could it be that it is the lost capacity for unadulterated vision that furnishes those suspended moments, because we saw then with an immediacy that we have since lost?

My suspended moments are almost all focused on the house, or the garden. The stomach ache would have been no unusual occurrence – most Europeans in Egypt were mildly ill a good deal of the time, and at risk of typhoid, dysentery, sand-fly fever, malaria and a few other plagues. Any cut, bite or scratch became infected. All such abrasions were treated with iodine, which stung and left yellowish-brown stains, or mercurochrome, which was a gaudy red. I carried this war-paint all the time, especially around the knees, charting the injuries of the previous days.

My bed, and the mosquito net, were in the night nursery. Lucy slept there too. Across the passage was the day nursery, in which we lived. The passage reached from one end of the house to the other, and rooms opened off it to either side, like a hotel corridor – a peculiar arrangement for domestic architecture, but then it was an unusual house, or at least unlike anything I have known since. Externally, it was cream stucco with green shutters, flat-roofed and with a wide covered veranda running round most of two sides. The front door was rather grandly porticoed, with a flight of steps leading up. Now, it seems to me like a small version of one of those plantation mansions of the American deep south. It had been built in the early years of the century, along with its two neighbours, each of them lavishly surrounded by gardens and sharing an access driveway screened by a high hedge.

At the far end of that long corridor upstairs was our bathroom, which was also the visitors' bathroom, and outside its window was a palm tree in which lived an owl, which would bob up and down in a strange private gymnastic performance. This was the Egyptian Little Owl, I had been told, and I always thought of it thus, with precision (heralding maybe an adult enthusiasm for extremely amateur ornithology). Next to the bathroom was Lucy's pantry, in which she had a primus stove and did small-scale cooking operations in areas over which she did not trust the kitchen servants, such as boiling the milk. On one legendary occasion one of the bottles of milk delivered daily had been found to contain a small live fish – indicating that whoever bottled or delivered it was in the habit of topping it up from the canal.

Next to the pantry was our bedroom, and then the spare bedroom, and opposite was the big nursery, with the flowered chintz sofa on which I languished when ailing. The nursery opened on to a veranda – the roof of the covered veranda around the ground floor. In very hot weather my parents slept on this veranda in a sort of large fruit cage. I never got to do this, and it was a focal point of dissatisfaction. Why not? Why them and not me? Strictly speaking, it was not even their territory, which was the big suite of bedroom, dressing-room and bathroom at the far end of the corridor into which I seldom penetrated. Occasionally I was allowed in to explore the contents of my mother's jewellery box or to watch her apply her make-up. I perceived their quarters as qualitatively different from ours, more richly furnished and full of lavish smells (my mother's scent, my father's leather shoes) but I always felt a touch displaced there and was quite happy to retreat again. Next to the nursery was a further guest bedroom, a sliver of a room reserved for bachelors, of which there was a plentiful supply, an unending stream of Eighth Army buccaneers on leave from the Western Desert. My parents were extremely gregarious; there was always someone staying, lunch parties and tea parties and 'people for drinks' were the norm.

The front door opened on to a large hall dominated at one end by a fireplace in which a fire was lit at Christmas, for ceremonial purposes. There was a Knole settee from which I was banned because I might bounce on it or dirty the cover: I cannot set eyes on a Knole settee, to this day, without a feeling of truculence, the submerged resentment of the *hoi polloi*. There was also an early nineteenth-century tallboy with brass handles in which were kept objects of importance: my father's papers, photograph albums. I was forbidden, equally, to open these drawers. The tallboy had a definite aura: it signified official, adult concerns. Today, that tallboy stands in my bedroom in London. It houses some of my clothes, and a fair amount of detritus like surplus Christmas wrapping paper and discarded spectacles. This seems to me a nice instance of the way in which a portentous inanimate object eventually gets its come-uppance, though in another sense I still have a respect for the tallboy – it has twice navigated the Mediterranean, it has an impenetrable past going back at least a hundred years before I first knew it, and it is all set to outlast me, for sure.

My parents evidently shipped furniture out to Egypt. The drawing-room and the dining-room, large formal rooms opening off the hall, were furnished in similar style. The only Middle Eastern touches I remember were the khelim and Turkish rugs on the floors and the Crusader sword that hung over the mantelpiece in the hall. Was it really a Crusader sword? It was a sword all right, and on a further occasion of family legend one of the resident Western Desert buccaneers was supposed to have snatched it up and cut off the head of a cobra found sunning itself on the front doorstep.

Just inside the front door was a little suite of rooms — bedroom, bathroom and pantry — inhabited by Nunn. Nunn was an elderly British expatriate who had come with the house, in some curious way. He was vaguely employed as a caretaker, and ministered to the generator which supplied our electricity. He was a small irascible man with a bristly white moustache who always wore a khaki bush jacket and a solar topi (this last was a touch outdated by then in Egypt) and passed his time haranguing the servants and the gardeners in a mixture of kitchen Arabic and army invective. He was taciturn and irritable and a stern misogynist. He ignored Lucy and me as well as, for the most part, my mother. I only remember him talking at any length to my father.

Nunn now seems to me a strange and tragic figure. Who on earth was he? Tradition had it that he had fought in the Boer War and then somehow got washed up in Egypt on the way home. Certainly he had some sort of army background. There he is, in my head, always carrying a fly-whisk, standing in the front drive bawling out Ali, one of the gardeners, inhabiting a limbo of his own in which he was not one of us but neither was he exactly an employee. Now I see his irascibility as stemming from frustration and loneliness, his xenophobia as an expression of his own social insecurity. And there is a further Nunn-related moment which comes swimming up. Late in the war, he is no longer at Bulaq Dakhrur. He has gone, though I seem not to have noticed the moment of his going. Lucy and I go to visit him in Cairo. He is lying in a chair in a stuffy, over-furnished room, suddenly old and ill, tended by two young women who, it comes across to me, are his daughters. And they are not English. Lucy, wearing a pinched look, says that they are Lebanese. The misogyny cannot have been so total after all.

Behind a screen in the far corner of the hall was the entrance to the pantry and the kitchen, of intense interest to me because largely out of bounds. There was the pantry, in which Nunn ate his solitary meals and my mother gave daily orders to Hassan, the cook. Beyond that was the kitchen proper, which was absolutely forbidden territory. I doubt if my mother had ever been there. It was a mysterious, noisy, smelly place from which came sounds of raucous laughter, quarrels, commotion. Its activities spilled out on to the back door steps and the area around, which was discreetly fenced off from the drive by bushes. Here the servants sat to talk, to prepare vegetables, wash things in enamel basins, pluck chickens. I was not allowed to go there either but I did, on occasion. I would creep through the bushes and sit in fascination, watching and listening. Hassan, Abdul, Daoud and whoever else there was would kindly turn a blind eye. They knew I was out of order, but were prepared to collude. They weren't much interested probably. I was only a child, and a girl at that.

And thus I squat in the dust, unconsciously imitating the way in which Abdul and Hassan sit, and listen to their conversation which I cannot understand, except for odd words here and there. And so, today, at some deep level, the sound of spoken Arabic is still homely and familiar. I watch Hassan's deft fingers flying over the carcass of a chicken, I study the complexity of his face with its ritual gashes on the cheeks, deep grooves on the plum-dark skin. Hassan is from Nubia, as is Daoud, the tall spindly *suffragi*. Hassan is nice – he smiles and laughs. Mansour, the head gardener, is dour and grim. I am nervous of him and keep well out of his way. He once saw me snapping off poinsettia heads and shopped me to my mother. There was a great row and I was banned from that part of the garden.

All these people have strong and definite personalities for me. Abdul, the head *suffragi*, is a figure of status and authority; he is grave but also kindly. I take him very seriously and always do what he says. Daoud, on the other hand, is a clown – he fools about. He invites horseplay and repartee. Hassan is amiable and jokey. Mansour is unapproachable and not to be trusted. Ahmed is the garden boy; he is my friend. I am in a relationship with each of these which is unlike my relationship with anyone else – with the family, or with my parents' friends. It is an intimate one, but is also somehow bewildering. I do not know quite where I am.

I realize now how this mirrors the Victorian or Edwardian household in which children and servants exist in a stratum of their own, locked into a relationship rich with ambiguities. The world of Ivy Compton-Burnett and, most accurately of all, of Lewis Carroll. I have always warmed to that interpretation which sees Alice's anarchic vision as an attempt to penetrate the confusing codes of an adult world in which the roles of adults themselves are shifty and unreliable – authoritative at one moment, servile at the next. Reading today of the White Rabbit or the Red Queen, I see myself sitting in the bushes outside the kitchen door at Bulaq Dakhrur, observing Abdul and Hassan and Mansour.

I have met up with Ahmed in the place behind the bamboo clump, both of us in flight from authority – I from Lucy, he from Mansour.

'I dare you to eat earth,' says Ahmed. 'Look . . .'

He scoops up a handful of earth, grinning. He crams it into his mouth.

I watch, stonily, waiting for him to expire. He does not. 'Now you,' challenges Ahmed, grinning hugely.

I am in a fix. If I do it, I will surely die. If I do not, I shall lose face, irrevocably.

There is really no choice. I gather a handful of earth, shove it into my mouth. My teeth grind on the gritty bits. I swallow.

Ahmed would have been about twelve, I think. Certainly

he was not much taller than I was (there would have been good reason for that) and his voice had not broken. He was Mansour's minion, employed to fetch and carry and to do those tasks beneath the dignity of Mansour and Ali. Most of his time was spent sweeping paths in a desultory way, with bursts of frenzied activity whenever Mansour hove into view. And the earth-eating episode is again of course embellished with a touch of hindsight. The conversation cannot have run quite like that – there was a language barrier. Suffice it that we understood each other perfectly.

This infrastructure of service seems astonishing, for one small family. It was in no way unusual. All European families would have had one or two or more servants. So, equally, would Egyptian families of any prosperity at all. The bulk of the population were *fellaheen*; most of those who were not were engaged in ministering to the merchant and administrative classes, whether foreign or indigenous. Again, it seems more like another century than another place.

Beyond the house, and all around it, was the garden, which was largely my mother's creation. I suspect that an addiction to gardening is genetic. My maternal grandmother was a dedicated gardener, and had created a memorable garden in West Somerset, strongly influenced by Gertrude Jekyll. My mother made an equally distinguished garden in Egypt. Now I have the fever, though without their resources of time and space, and so has my daughter. The gardens have become increasingly modest, down the generations, but the obsession continues. The Bulaq Dakhrur garden was unashamedly English in design – it had lawns and a lily pond with a willow, pergolas and formal beds and a rose garden. But the flowers were zinnias and canna lilies and poinsettias, the shrubs were lantana and plumbago and bougainvillaea. There was a long pergola over an intersecting brick path and a round pergola above a concrete basin with a bronze statue of Mercury in the middle.

The Mercury basin is empty of water. It is cracked, making the surface uneven, and there is a scum of leaves in the bottom. I ride my bicycle round and round it, as around a Wall of Death at a fun-fair. This is thrilling and hazardous – there is always the risk of falling off.

Looking at a photograph of the Mercury basin, it seems to me that the diameter is only some five or six feet. A small bicycle, it must have been. A small child. My perspective of that space is dizzily distorted. I see it with double vision – the reality of the photograph in front of me, and that inward eye which insists upon a sweeping expanse, a great curve around which I hurtle. Both, though, are accurate. It is I who am the inconstant feature.

There was a water garden – a shady place with channels and bridges and a central island thick with bamboo. This was a particular haven of mine. There were frogs and tadpoles and goldfish and the whole place lent itself perfectly to complex naval games with craft made out of bits of plank nailed together which I played with my friend and neighbour Steven Hurst.

The Hursts lived next door. Steven's father worked for the Egyptian government as Director General of the Ministry of Irrigation. Their large garden adjoined ours. Steven was a year older than me, and together we led a rich and creative life in this extended territory, based on an expedient pooling of our respective skills. I was good at inventing the games we should play; Steven excelled at making the requisite props. I devised the naval game; Steven acquired planks, nails and a hammer – illicitly no doubt – and made the ships. There was another elaborate game which centred on a wooden packing-case. This involved bows and arrows – also made by Steven – and had overtones of pioneer life. Goodness knows what was the inspiration for this. A photograph records this activity. There we are, sitting outside our packing-case house, Steven on a chair holding the bow, me on the ground holding the arrow (as squaw, presumably). We both look rather cross, and I know why, because I remember the taking of the photograph. We had been made to stop what we were doing and pose; we resented the interruption. And once again there is an unnerving conflict between what is in my head and what I see in this old photograph. There, I see two quite small children and an upturned packing-case. But memory supplies something entirely different – an impression of mature preoccupation, of significant business rudely broken into by importunate outsiders. And the packing-case is not a packing-case but a house. It has doors and windows and furnishings, smoke comes from the chimney. Outside, the buffalo roam. Or something of the kind. At any rate, I know that the camera lies. It is not thus at all.

Steven and his family left Egypt in 1941, long before we did. Another family moved in next door, with children somewhat younger than I was who could not offer a substitute for that creative relationship. Throughout the 1940s I was distinctly short on companionship. I had a bonanza in the summer, on the beaches of Alexandria, but for the rest of the year I only saw other children when my mother drove Lucy and me in to Cairo and left us at Gezira Sporting Club for the afternoon, where we made hay for a few hours – Lucy indulging in a good gossip with her friends and I rampaging with their charges. Very occasionally special friends came out to Bulaq Dakhrur. Margaret, who was my age exactly, with plaits and pink cheeks. And an exuberant small Irish boy called Peter, richly freckled and, according to Lucy, uncontrollable. I was much taken with Peter. Once, he came to stay and we were allowed to sleep in adjacent beds. Lucy put the light out, with awful admonitions that there was to be no talking and no getting out of bed. After a few minutes, I heard a rhythmic creaking and squeaking. Peter had discovered the possibilities of determined bouncing on the spring bedstead which was topped only by a thin flock mattress. I had never thought of this. I too bounced. We bounced in unison until Lucy erupted from the nursery, looking thunder.

But this was an exceptional event. For the most part I was significantly alone, thrown on to my own resources of communion with trees and guinea-pigs backed up by a practised system of internal fantasy. After Steven left, the packing-case house fell into disuse and the water-garden navy rotted away. But there is a curious coda to our relationship, involving the sort of coincidence that no novelist would be allowed to get away with. Life is far more fortuitous than fiction.

We lost touch entirely. In 1975 I was living in a village outside Oxford with my husband and children. Attached to our sixteenth-century farmhouse was a tithe barn, then semi-derelict and the property of a local farmer. We heard that this barn had been sold to a sculptor, who was intending to restore it and live and work there. One day there was a knock at the door – our future neighbour had called by to introduce himself. It was Steven – now metamorphosed into the sculptor Steve Hurst. And thus we became next-door neighbours and friends all over again, half a world away and half a lifetime on.

We had a swimming-pool at Bulaq Dakhrur. This sounds grander than it in fact was. The swimming-pool was a rectangle of raised concrete, just big enough and deep enough for an adult to dive into without hitting the bottom or the other side. It had murky green depths and a permanent scum of eucalyptus pollen. A jocular Eighth Hussar had once spent a morning persuading me that there was a Nile catfish down there ('Great big fellow – felt his whiskers against my leg . . .') and on one occasion a little snake came whipping through the eucalyptus pollen towards me while Lucy, who couldn't swim, keened in dismay from the edge. I yearned for the glimmering turquoise wastes of the pool at Gezira Sporting Club, with its tiers of diving boards and ripe miasma of Nivea cream.

The drive which led past the big lawn to the house was lined on one side with immensely tall eucalyptus trees. The maintenance of it all occupied Mansour, Ali and Ahmed day in and day out the year round and its survival depended, like the surrounding fields, on the periodic release of water from the canal system. Once a month the banks of the ditch which bordered our property on one side were breached in several places by Ali – always a dramatic and ceremonial business – and the brown waters gushed out all over the garden, inundating it to a depth of a couple of inches. 'The flood', this ritual event was called – and in my mind it was associated inextricably with the biblical Flood, which I imagined to have been similar, if a bit deeper. I was confined to the veranda and the paths until the waters sank, bitterly watching Ahmed who sploshed around barefoot in the glorious cool mud, grinning complacently at me.

Once a year a further ritual took place – an esoteric form of spring-cleaning. The snake charmer came. He was brought out from Cairo by my father in the car and immediately taken off to be thoroughly searched – a demeaning procedure much relished by the servants, who carried it out, and in no way objected to by the snake charmer, who expected it. Everybody knew – the snake charmer included – that inferior practitioners arrived with their quarry concealed about their persons, to be produced with a flourish at the appropriate moment. To submit with dignity to the search was simply to make the point that he was not of this order. And then, the search over, he got going – followed by the entire household in a Pied Piper procession, my parents, Lucy and myself, any guests invited out for the spectacle, all the servants. It was a festival, as well as a necessary purgation.

He began with the garden. He walked ahead of us, chanting softly, apparently to himself. He would pause, consider. He would continue, pause again. The chanting would get louder. And then he would shoot a skinny brown arm out of the sleeve of his galabiya up into the foliage of the pergola, or on to the overhanging branch of a tree, and there would be a snake, whipping and thrashing in his grasp. The snake would be encouraged to slash at his sleeve with its fangs – to drain the poison, I imagine – and was then dropped into the sack tied to his waist. And on we went, with everyone speculating sagely as to how it was done. He smelled them out, being endowed with some extra sense inconceivable to the rest of us. He mesmerized them with the chanting, forcing them to rustle and betray their presence. He was in collusion with the servants, who had planted the snakes half an hour previously (this last suggested by cynical visitors and hotly refuted by my parents). I still don't know the secret of it, but it happened, and was vastly satisfying to all concerned. Except, I dare say, the snakes.

Having cleansed the garden, the snake charmer would then ask to go into the house. My mother would say that it was quite out of the question that there were any snakes in the house. The snake charmer would insist that he knew that there were. We would go inside. And then the real fun began. The snake charmer proceeded from room to room, intoning. The chanting would become louder and faster. My mother's 'I told you so' expression would change to one of incredulity. On different occasions snakes were produced from the cupboard under the stairs, the record cabinet and, memorably, from under our bath.

I was entranced by snakes and impervious to warnings. The most serious erosion of all freedoms, in my view, was the rule that you could never go barefoot in the desert because of sand-vipers. Even now, the feeling of sand on bare feet has for me an extra dimension of sybaritic delight. Many of our garden snakes would have been venomous to a greater or lesser degree, but I spent much time hunting for them – unsuccessfully for the most part – and yearned most of all for a sighting of a cobra, rumoured still to exist in small numbers in Lower Egypt. There had after all been the Crusader sword episode; next time, I wanted to be on the spot. The ultimate treat of the snake charmer's visits was that I would be allowed to keep a small harmless snake. I would carry it about in the pocket of my dress for days, ignoring Lucy's revulsion and admonitions, until the poor thing escaped.

We went in to Cairo only once a week, sometimes less often. The garden was my universe. I knew every inch of it and was involved in innumerable private communions. There were the places where I hid myself – the bamboo patch on the pond island, the hummock of vine branches in the hedge by the swimming-pool. There were favoured plants and bushes: the arum lilies by the pond with their thick central tubes which could be illicitly snapped off and made into a sort of pencil, the fat buds of the fuchsias which could be popped. But the eucalyptus trees in the drive were the most crucial of all. I knew each one intimately – the smooth trunks from which the bark would peel in strips, the long crisp greenish-blue leaves which smelled of eucalyptus if you scrunched them in your hand, the little conical seeds which released that powdery dust. The central and tallest tree had a large misshapen lump a foot or so across on its trunk, at about my head height. This seemed to imbue it with some mystical power. I revered this tree. I communed with it, most definitely. I would sit for hours between its spreading roots, telling it things. I complained to it, and went to it for consolation and reassurance.

The capacity for animistic belief lies deep. I find it extremely interesting, but only in an anthropological or mythological sense. I am a hard-headed woman now-adays and would not be able to read the works of W. H. Hudson or Richard Jeffries without wincing. I cannot now imagine having a relationship with a tree other than an environmentally protective one or one of aesthetic pleasure. Nevertheless, there lurks within me somewhere the spirit of a person who once quite naturally and unquestioningly communed with a thirty-foot eucalyptus tree.

Solitary children are no doubt even more prone than others to seek animistic solace. I communed also with an array of animals – principally my collection of tortoises and a large herd of guinea-pigs. The guinea-pigs were satisfying as well in another and far less mystical way. I was a child reared on the King James Version of the Bible, especially the Old Testament. Guinea-pigs breed with biblical intensity – they will descend unto the fourth generation within a year. I saw mine as an intri-guing biological expression of the proceedings of the Old Testament and charted their genealogies accordingly – who begat whom all laid out neatly in a family tree on the nursery wall, with ruled lines and my best writing. Though the orderly effect was muddied here and there by outbreaks of rampant incest. The guinea-pigs were individually named, with groupings of names to indicate families – admirals for one lot, Nelson, Drake, Jellicoe and so on – contemporary aircraft for a cadet line, Spitfire, Hurricane, Liberator. I wonder now why I didn't carry things to a logical conclusion and plunder the Old Testament for names; probably Lucy balked at that – there would have been implications of blasphemy.

Most young children take a pretty animistic line where domestic pets are concerned. For a number of years I was one of the judging panel for the largest children's creative-writing competition in this country and came to realize that the central concern of the nation's under-eight-year-olds is hamsters. Cats and dogs came next, with budgies doing quite well too. And the writing quite often suggested not only an attribution of human responses, but a distinct emotional need. Animals had a role: they were surrogates, or icons. I'm not so sure about trees. My particular tendency to relate to the surroundings seems perhaps the personal solution of an extremely solitary child – no siblings, the company of other children exceptional rather than normal. But it still remains part of a general capacity, an ability to fuse with the physical world which we lose in adult life just as we lose that capacity for intense and unadulterated observation. Does this then mean that animistic belief is childlike or that children have an insight into some primal state of unity with the natural world?

Chapter Three

When I was very young I was under the impression that Lucy had a large black hole in the middle of her chest – a belief inspired I imagine by glimpses of that shadowed cleft between a woman's breasts. Lucy was decorous to the point of prudishness. I certainly never saw her naked, although we shared a bedroom. Her dressing and undressing was a deft and skilful business – there was never so much as the flash of a bare limb. The black hole impressed me but I did not find it in any way strange, though I was well aware that my mother did not have one, nor any of the other women I saw frequently in bathing costumes. I simply took it that Lucy was more distinguished anatomically, as she was more distinguished in every other way, so far as I was concerned.

My father, less adroit than Lucy, once let a bathing towel slip so that for an instant I glimpsed what seemed to be a distinctly odd arrangement around the base of his torso. This did not particularly interest me, but I thought in a detached way that perhaps he had seaweed growing out of him. Again, nothing to wonder at.

One of the problems with this assemblage of slides in the head is that they cannot be sorted chronologically. All habits are geared towards the linear, the sequential, but memory refuses such orderliness. Without internal evidence of some kind there is no way of knowing what happened when, or what comes before something else. Here, though, there does seem to me to be some distinct internal evidence. It is only very small children – under four or five – who retain this wonderfully surreal vision. It is an anarchic vision, too. They are seeing the world without preconceptions or expectations, and therefore anything is possible. There is no reason why a woman should not have a black hole in the middle of her chest, or a man sprout seaweed from his body. It is the unlicensed vision that later finds its way into kinds of fiction, the fantasy that allows a woman to turn into a tree or a man into a beetle. But this is the sophisticated fantasy that springs from a knowledge of the boundaries of possibility – the child's view is the very opposite. It arises because of absence of expectation, not a manipulation of what is known.

Children arrive soon enough at rationality. At some point I no longer saw that black hole; at some point both the hole and the seaweed gave way to an awareness of and curiosity about sexuality. But that original perception lingers as ghostly evidence of another lost capacity.

Is it, though, entirely lost? I have always found an eerie resonance in the surrealism of dreams. Here again, you walk a landscape in which things are not as they are in the world you know, and yet you suspend disbelief. Nothing is surprising; nothing is impossible. Here is a recent such experience. I am at a social gathering – some bookish gathering. I stand beside a fireplace in which a number of people are lying stacked like logs. They are mainly poets, including several that I know personally. I am talking to a literary editor of my acquaintance. I see that the area around his eyes is covered with flakes of oatmeal, attached to cobwebs, it seems. His eye cavities are also filled with oatmeal. None of this disturbs me, any more than do the stacked poets.

Some may prefer to interpret this as a view of literary editors, or of poets. I see it simply as a nice instance of the anarchism of dreams – a refreshing escape from the dictation of reality. The only parallel experience seems to be those rare surviving snatches of very early observation, before the view of the world was made for ever inflexible by the impositions of knowledge. I do not of course mean by this that I am against knowledge. Obviously to retain that vision, or any other of these early ways of seeing, would be to be in some way crippled. What seems valuable is the way in which their retention even in such frustratingly incomplete form is perhaps an insight into the way in which children perceive the world.

Moreover, in this instance the way of seeing provides also a clue to when the seeing was done. The whole package of these momentary views supplies the basic evidence, and the framework, for this book. But it is recalcitrant evidence, because it is untethered. Each item floats free in time, making it impossible to marshal them into any sort of order. The best that can be done is to look at each one and see what it seems to say about how this particular child saw things, and then investigate what it was that she saw. And sometimes it will also be possible to slot each view into a proper chronological place and say – that happened just about then, or then.

Perhaps I was three when I saw the black hole and the seaweed. Somewhat older when having those thoughts about time at the beginning of the book – six or seven. In both instances the deduction about age is made possible by the internal evidence of the process of thought. Other moments are placeable because of other kinds of evidence – firm historical evidence, sometimes. A great deal was going on at the time, after all, and sometimes it is possible to fix my own glimpse within the historical narrative. In this chapter I want to do just that – take the shards within my head and try to place them within the correct strata. And try to see what light if any this view casts on what I now know was going on.

I am in the garden of the villa in Alexandria that my mother has rented for the summer. Trench and Walker have come for lunch, and soon we will be going to the beach, to Sidi Bishr. Trench and Walker are naval officers. I find them dashing and sophisticated; I admire them immensely. I am behaving badly, showing off like crazy and uneasily aware that I will catch it from Lucy later on. Someone is taking a photo of us, and I have snatched up the uniform cap of Trench, or of Walker, and put it on.

And there I am indeed, in the photo, wearing the naval cap, flanked by these two young men in their white drill uniforms. Very young men. Eighteen, they look – twenty at a pinch. I am scowling. An insufferable child, from the look of me.

Once again, the view of things has a double exposure. I see those two figures twice over – they are of a maturity that is unreachable and impressive, and they are boys. And alongside that double vision there lies the haunting impression of having been told that one or both of them subsequently died in action.

When eventually I came to write a novel – *Moon Tiger* – part of which was concerned with the Libyan campaign and wartime Cairo, I found that this superseded vision lurked all the time behind the books that I read and the film and photographs at which I looked. Now, I saw the faces of very young men – boys waving from the backs of trucks, making the V-sign, driving tanks, humping equipment. But there was also that other, equally credible image of an inaccessible maturity. Both views informed the book, in the end.

By the end of 1941 there were over 140,000 British troops stationed in and around Cairo, and three-quarters of a million in the Middle East. To these were added the

Australians, the New Zealanders, South Africans, a scattering of Canadians, Free French, Greeks, Poles — the streets of both Cairo and Alexandria were awash with soldiers, the Delta roads and the desert road from Cairo to Alexandria were jammed with army convoys. This invasion was received with mixed feelings. Those Egyptians whose memories reached back to the First World War and the excesses of some troops, especially the Australians, quailed. Indeed, so fervent were some of these memories that at the outset of the war all Australians were stationed in Palestine, at the insistence of the government. Egypt remained neutral, on the advice of the British government, and while Egyptians were glad to have the Italians kept at bay and ultimately disposed of most were clear that this was not, in the last resort, their war. But the fact remained that its arrival on Egypt's doorstep transformed the country. An army has to be serviced. From 1940 until British forces finally left North Africa much of the country's available resources were committed to the supply and maintenance of this huge influx of population and its requirements, with all that that implies. Some grew fat on it; others suffered.

For the British community it was on the whole a welcome incursion, except in that it was of course accompanied by the possibility of Egypt falling to Rommel. The patriotic duty to receive and entertain the troops was no imposition on people like my parents — it provided a stimulating extension to the social round. Bulaq Dakhrur saw a continuous stream of Eighth Army visitors. In the Alexandrian summers my mother enlivened the afternoons at the beach by taking along young naval officers or whoever else was around. I have to say that I cannot remember much entertainment of other ranks. British Cairo retained the rigid social structure it had always known. Officers only were allowed to join Gezira Sporting Club and the Turf Club.

For Egyptians, this was their first exposure to members of the British working class *en masse*. For the vast majority of them, the only British they came across were professionals of one kind or another – government officials, engineers, teachers, people working for the oil companies and industrial concerns. Troops had been there in the First World War, of course, but in smaller numbers. Now, they were receiving them in hordes: mostly very young, many of them overseas for the first time in their lives. They too were undergoing cultural shock, and many could not cope, displaying a xenophobia and racialism that perhaps differed only from that of the professional classes in being more explicit and more openly expressed. The only two words of Arabic that most soldiers knew were *yalla* and *imshi* – succinct versions of 'go away'. For many urban Egyptians there were of course rich pickings. A bonanza for the tourist industry, for the shops and cafés, for the street traders and the craftsmen in the Mouski, for the prostitutes of the Birka. For the rest, one can only think that whole experience must have been dismaying, and revealing.

I was in something of the same position as the average

PL in front of the Mercury fountain – the basin filled with water at this point

Above: A desert picnic. *Left to right:* Lucy, PL, her mother and a friend. Note the essential props of rug and Thermos

Below: Steven Hurst and PL outside their packing-case house

PL leaping into Alexandria harbour, aged five – gourds attached to waist to prevent drowning

Above: Lucy with PL in 1943

Above left: Tea on a houseboat in Alexandria harbour in 1937. PL with her father. The design of the Marmite label does not seem to have changed significantly in over fifty years

Below left: The swimming pool at Bulaq Dakhrur – PL's mother with a friend. The wooden contraptions to the left are guinea-pig hutches

Above: Staff portrait on the front steps of Bulaq Dakhrur. Nunn in the centre with his dog Fly. The tall figure on the extreme left is Daoud, with Hassan the cook next to him, and then Abdul, the head *suffragi*. On Nunn's left is Ali, the gardener. The others I cannot identify

Below: Alexandria 1940. PL with naval officers

PL with *fellaheen* children near Bulaq Dakhrur. A deeply
disquieting photo in its brutal contrasts, with the baby donkey as
the cosy feature of interest

PL and her father at Sidi Bishr No. 2. The beach stand-pipe seems a surprising luxury

Egyptian. I too had known only one kind of British person. Now I too discovered that English is spoken in many different ways, and that there were apparently mysterious gradations of Englishness which appeared in some perverse way to mirror Lucy's definition of degrees of non-Englishness. It was bewildering. My previous indoctrination had been that English was an exclusive club. If you spoke English you were a member of the club, and that was the end of it. Now I discovered – slowly and incompetently – that things weren't quite like that after all. It was more complicated, and bafflingly so. I was quite devoid of the innate social perceptions of any home-bred British child. I had not acquired them by the time I came to England in early adolescence, and was to continue to commit what were seen by my relatives as solecisms and gross errors of judgement.

The soldiers at the searchlight battery have given me some moths which have been killed by flying into the light. Wonderful moths – some of them several inches across, with wings patterned like rich tapestry. Lucy and I make these moths the subject of our Natural History period, during lessons. We would like to know their names but are frustrated because we have no Egyptian moth book. As an attempt at classification, I try to make crayon drawings of them, and become exasperated because I am so bad at this. My drawings have no bearing at all upon the glowing reality. The searchlight soldiers are nice – it is always a treat to walk over the fields to visit them. Lucy takes them cakes that Hassan has made, and has given each of them one of her housewives.

Plenty of internal evidence here. This is probably sometime in 1942, before the battle of Alamein. The searchlight battery would not otherwise have been positioned in the fields near Bulaq Dakhrur, where it was presumably part of the Cairo defence system, though the city was never in fact bombed, unlike Alexandria. Also, my preoccupations over the moths show that Lucy has by now turned from nurse into governess, of which much more anon.

Those manning the searchlight battery were a small group – three or four, I think – leading a solitary life out there in the cultivation, and a leisurely one too for the most part, presumably. Once, Lucy got me up after I had been put to bed to see a plane caught like a firefly in the crossed beams of two searchlights – one of them ours, maybe. She was wildly excited, and wanted to see it shot down: I was surprised and perturbed by this uncharacteristic bloodlust. If there were searchlights there must also have been anti-aircraft guns somewhere not too far away, but I don't remember either seeing or hearing these. And since there were no raids, what was that plane doing pinned in the beams? A reconnaissance plane, perhaps, or not a German aircraft at all.

The searchlight soldiers did not form part of those groups drinking whisky and soda on the Bulaq Dakhrur lawn in the dusk, nor of those larky lunchtime bathing parties on the rickety wooden platform with benches alongside our pool. This seemed to me slightly odd – they were after all our neighbours, in a sense. They were English, weren't they? If ever I queried this omission, I cannot remember the justification. But Lucy and I visited them, bestowing cakes and housewives and receiving in return dead moths and genial chat. One of the solders says he has a little girl just my age back at home. I overhear him remark to Lucy that it is a shame, me growing up in a place like this. I am astonished by this comment, and mildly offended.

A housewife (pronounced hussif), for those mystified, was a sewing-kit constructed out of a length of cloth fitted with pockets in which were tucked scissors, needles and thread, buttons, darning requisites and so forth, which was then rolled up and neatly tied with tapes. Lucy was an excellent seamstress; she made these things in batches and presented them to favoured visitors. My impression of the British army was of a feckless lot forever in trouble with their buttons and their socks.

Alamein is sixty miles from Alexandria. By the time of the fall of Tobruk and Rommel's thrust to the Egyptian border and beyond we were that close to the prospect of German occupation. I come now to what seems, in retrospect, one of the more incomprehensible aspects of recollection. It does not seem to me that there was then, or at any other point, any atmosphere of panic, apprehension or even of general unease. It is possible that adult feelings of this kind simply did not filter through to me, or that I was carefully shielded. Somehow, I don't think that was the case. Children are sensitive to adult anxieties. If adults are abstracted or preoccupied by worry or fear, they know. I don't remember my parents, or Lucy, being overtly concerned. Life went on just as it always had done. My father went to his office (he had not been able to join up because of extremely poor eyesight); my mother supervised the house and garden, went into Cairo a couple of times a week to shop and go to the Club, and did some mild war work. She helped in the offices of an organization called SSAFA – the Soldiers', Sailors' and Airmen's Family Association, which liaised between members of the armed forces and their families back home, and she visited convalescent troops in the army hospital. I occasionally accompanied her and her friends as they tried to interest these men in something called Occupational Therapy. I distinctly recall embroidery frames and raffia kits – received, one would assume, with some derision. But the war seems to have affected us mainly as an extension of social opportunity, and a vaguely disquieting offstage rumble. I remember jocular speculation: the rumour that Rommel had earmarked Bulaq Dakhrur as a convenient out-of-town headquarters, the assurance that our dogs would be well treated because they were dachshunds.

It seems a bizarre insouciance, now. In 1942 it must have been apparent to any reasonably shrewd observer that things could go either way, and indeed that a good deal pointed to the imminent fall of Egypt to the advancing German army. Mass raids on Cairo and an aerial invasion like that of Crete were both anticipated in June 1942. Cairo was a hotbed of rumour and gossip, all of which must have meant that official apprehensions of this kind percolated to the rest of the community. And to some extent they undoubtedly did. The wives and families of military personnel had been required to leave for Palestine or South Africa some while before, in August 1940. Some civilian families had gone, but most had not, and nor did they until the fall of Tobruk at the end of June precipitated what was known both then and subsequently as 'The Flap'. Even the terminology is significant – dismissive and a touch contemptuous. The Embassy and GHQ burned their files till, allegedly, the ash rained down on Cairo. Now at last there was a serious run on the trains to Palestine.

And about time too, one may think. It is hard to diagnose the sources of what now seems a combination of intransigence and a determination not to face facts. It is an attitude perfectly portrayed in J. G. Farrell's novel *The Singapore Grip*, in which the incredulity of the British community in Singapore in the face of the Japanese invasion, and the defiant fiddling as the place began to burn, are seen as a manifestation of imperial confidence. Not only did the sun never set on the Empire, but it was inconceivable that it would ever do so. Well, Egypt was not part of the Empire, but it was very much a part of the global British presence. The behaviour and attitudes of Farrell's characters reflect for me the general impression that came across to a child in Egypt in what must have appeared the equally hazardous days of the summer of 1942. Which makes Farrell's fictional achievement the more impressive: he had not been present in Singapore in any incarnation.

We joined the run for the railway station and the trains to Palestine. And I remember practically nothing. Certainly no sense of panic, nor any suggestion that we might not be coming back. My father remained behind in Cairo. My mother, Lucy and I set off, initially I think in the company of other families, for what seems to have been seen as an unexpected change from the usual summer routine of removal to Alexandria. My mother had made inquiries about pleasant seaside resorts. She was an enthusiastic traveller and had been frustrated the previous year in a whim to go to Cyprus for the summer when it was pointed out by my father that this might not be the most sensible move in 1941. A month or two in Palestine was not seen as any great inconvenience.

And in the event, of course, two or three months was all that it was, but I cannot see now how anyone can have been so confident at the time.

I had been in England when war broke out, and would be there again in time for VE day in 1945. In between lay the five most perilous years of the century, and my childhood. Lucy and I were at my grandmother's home in Somerset in September 1939. In August my grandmother had taken an extended family party to Chamonix in the French Alps – my uncle and his wife, my eldest cousin, a cousin of my mother's, my mother and Lucy and myself. It seems to have been planned as a final gathering and holiday while the going was good, and in retrospect appears a little misjudged. My father was still in Cairo, my aunt Rachel was in Somerset, receiving bland postcards from my grandmother extolling the scenery and saying how nice it was not to be getting any newspapers, in response to which Rachel fired back telegrams urging immediate scrutiny of the press. I remember collecting wortleberries and pottering a little way up mountains in a pair of real laced-up climbing boots. Eventually Rachel's telegrams found their mark and we dispersed in haste – my mother in a frenzied dash to Marseilles to try to get a boat to Egypt, the rest of us to England. My grandmother, Lucy and I arrived back in Somerset nicely in time to hear Chamberlain's speech on the wireless in the solemnity of the drawing-room at Golsoncott, with all the household summoned to sit in silence. Then, and only then, did the sense of adult anxiety reach me. Afterwards, Lucy and I went back up to the nursery and I played the record of 'The Teddy Bears' Picnic' on the wind-up gramophone, over and over again:

If you go down to the woods today, you'd better go in disguise
If you go down to the woods today, you're in for a big surprise.

The words thumped away in my head, an accompaniment to that portentous and disturbing group in the drawing-room, with a man's thin dry voice coming from the wireless and all the grown-ups wearing strange expressions. To this day, that tune is loaded with a sense of menace.

My grandmother immediately embarked on a battle by telegram with my parents. She wanted me to be left in England with her rather than risk the journey back to Egypt. My parents wanted me sent back, and won. Lucy and I set off in a party of British women and children on a complicated trek across Europe by land and sea. And I cannot but reflect, now, that Lucy need not have done this. She could have said, No, I prefer to see this war out in my own country – and handed in her notice. But she didn't. She took me to London, where we met up with the rest of the little clutch of fleeing expatriates, and embarked on a journey which is reduced for me now to an impression of crowded railway carriages, people talking French, and an abiding worry about the gas-mask which I had to carry and not lose on pain of instant death, or so I understood. And there is also a stubborn and perplexing image of a hotel bedroom with clanking radiators in which I lie and know that I am in Venice. Venice? The straightforward route would seem to have been down through France to Marseilles and thence by boat to Alexandria, a popular alternative to the sea trip from England to Egypt. But this determined inner voice proclaims – Venice. And inquiry reveals that this was indeed the case. Since Italy had not yet come into the war it was thought safer to go by train across France and Switzerland and then by ship down the Adriatic.

For a child, the world of public events is an irrelevant background clamour. And even when the clamour becomes so insistent as to direct the pattern of daily life, it is still accepted on the whole. It is only later on that we acquire the gall to quarrel with the malevolence of fate, and much good does it do. Children do indeed question the dictation of circumstance – why should I do this, that or the other – but when it comes to the huge manipulations of history they are silent, naturally enough. This is a part of the immutability of things. This is how it goes; there could be no other way. I accepted without surprise the flight down through Europe in October 1939, and the subsequent departure from Cairo to Palestine in June 1942. Both became, simply, part of an inevitable narrative. Except that even the narrative exists only because adult habits of mind impose one. At the time, there was no narrative – just the compelling immediacy of life.

The war was something which had stolen up and now was like some inescapable element. And yet it carried with it an implied chronology. After the war. When the war is over. My own nightly ritual of prayer suggested both chronology and the possibility of divine intercession: 'Please God, make the war end soon.' This I incanted, without examination. Equally, I moved drawing-pins around on the map of the Libyan desert which was stuck up on the wall, and charted the advance and retreat of the Eighth Army. I must have watched the line of drawing-pins creep back towards Cairo.

To follow now the course of the Western Desert campaign of 1941 and 1942 is to realize the extraordinary accelerated nature of time in war. So much happened so quickly. The initial British advance into Cyrenaica at the end of 1940, the turn of the tide with the arrival of Rommel and the German surge forward, the siege of Tobruk, the second allied offensive and the battle of Sidi Resegh, the renewed German thrust and fall of Tobruk, the battle of Alamein. Within twenty months or so the war had come and gone. It had been on the doorstep, and had then swept away over the horizon, become just a distant unstoppable clamour. But at the time, for those twenty months, it had roared in our ears. Even I had heard it, playing in the garden at Bulaq Dakhrur, walking the streets of Cairo with Lucy, seeing and listening to that khaki-clad horde.

But what I saw and heard seems nothing much to do with what I now know. Then, they were old and wise. Now they are so young, and I read with incredulity of boys straight from school who went out to train in the Delta and found themselves in the desert within months, commanding Crusader tanks. They must have shot from adolescence to an awful maturity. The language of Keith Douglas's brief memoir, *From Alamein to Zem Zem*, reflects something of this precarious fusion of forced sobriety and natural exuberance. He was twenty-two and was to be killed in the Normandy campaign.

For me, then, the war was not so much a sequence of events as a pervasive fact. And what was happening became fused with its backdrop. The desert. The desert swallowed up these people that I knew – these imposing figures who sprawled on the lawn at Bulaq Dakhrur, or joshed me into believing that there was a catfish in our swimming-pool – and then disgorged them again, weeks later. I knew the desert, of course. It was a place to which you went to have picnics. You drove out into it and searched out an overhang or a depression or some-where out of the wind and with a shred of shade, and then you spread a rug and got out the Thermoses and sandwiches. I knew favoured spots by name: Wadi Natrun, Wadi Digla. Wadis were best because they were periodic watercourses and so had minimal vegetation and, sometimes, flowers clinging to a crevice in the rocks or springing miraculously from the dry sand. I liked the desert. It was mysterious, apparently endless, and filled with treasure: little succulent plants, strange spiny trees, the trails of snakes and small creatures embroidered upon the sand. The solitary figures of Bedouin trekking along the skyline. Wind-rippled slopes down which you could roll. The desert, for me, meant Marmite sandwiches, milk in a Thermos and rewarding exploration.

And now the desert had a new significance. For one thing, it was no longer a single, infinite place. I had learned how the infinity out there could be tamed by a piece of paper: I knew what a map meant. I could see the desert in another way, reaching in brown wastes towards Tunisia in one direction and Palestine in the other. Those were the immensities in which the war roared, and into which vanished those I knew. It had become something voracious, and unreliable even in the most immediate sense. We continued to go for desert picnics, in 1940 and 1941 and 1942, but you could no longer go just anywhere. The desert had become vicious, sown with hazards by way of unexploded bombs and ammunition dumps. You could only go to designated safe zones, and even those could betray. A child my own age, the son of acquaintances of my parents, picked up a stick bomb and was fatally injured – an incident used by Olivia Manning in her Cairo trilogy in what seems one of the more insensitive translations of experience into fiction. The chill of this child's death reached me, in the garden at Bulaq Dakhrur. After that, the picnics in the desert ceased.

Underneath the house at Bulaq Dakhrur there was a cellar, used as a dump for superfluous objects: broken deck-chairs, my father's discarded golf-clubs, my old cot. It was a dry, musty place, always visited with caution because probably the haunt of snakes and scorpions. The floor of it, I remember, was sandy, as though the desert had thrust up here, a few feet below the surface of the garden.

And there, on that thin sand, I stand one day towards the end of the war. We are leaving Bulaq Dakhrur. The cellar is being turned out. Someone – my mother, Lucy – is overseeing the removal and disposal of what was there. This to be thrown out, that to be kept. And there in the corner is a little stack of kit-bags, and a tin trunk with a stencilled name on the lid. The kit-bags too have names, on tattered labels tied to their necks. They are the possessions of those the desert swallowed but did not disgorge. They have never returned to claim the stuff they left here till next time they came. And now no one knows what should be done with these things. They sit there in the corner of the cellar, on the sand, isolated.

Chapter Four

We are in the desert, somewhere outside Cairo. My mother has driven us to see what some archaeologists are doing, who are working out here in the middle of nowhere. The archaeologist to whom my mother talks is French. He is offering explanations, to which I do not listen. I see, simply.

I see a shallow scrape in the sand, a bowl in which lies in delicate relief a crouched skeletal outline. It is so faint that it seems to melt into the sand, or to be a pattern blown by the wind. There is the curve of the skull, the fan of ribs, the folded limbs. The trace of a hand. Perhaps I do listen to the explanation, with half an ear, because it comes to me as I stare that this is a person. Long, long ago, this was a person. It too saw, and felt, and thought. I stand there enthralled, glimpsing time, and death. I do not know what it is that I have seen, but I understand that it is of significance.

It was indeed. I have never forgotten. The moment appears seminal, and perhaps accounts for much.

It now seems to me that what I saw was a pre-

Dynastic burial. The precise details of a shallow bowl-like depression with a skeleton lying on its side in a foetal position accord nicely with descriptions of these very early cemeteries, and this one might have dated from any point between 5000 and 3000 BC. Such Neolithic communities lived in village settlements in both Upper and Lower Egypt. The dig we visited cannot have been far from Cairo – it would have been an afternoon excursion, or a day at the most. Possibly it was at the Fayoum, where there are very early pre-Dynastic sites, but the Fayoum is not conspicuously a desert area, and my recollection is very firmly of desert. Other possibilities are Merimda, and Maadi, just beyond Cairo.

When was this, then? My reactions do not seem to have been those of a very young child, but it would seem odd for archaeological activity of this kind to have been going on in the desert once the war had got going – I feel it cannot have been much later than 1940. So I was six or seven, and able to grasp the idea of immensities of time.

A necessary perception, in Egypt, but not one which I acquired in anything but the haziest way. My home-based education, administered by Lucy, was rigidly structured around books and a timetable supplied from England. Neither the system nor Lucy were flexible enough to take advantage of what lay all around us. When I see droves of primary school children in the Egyptian Hall of the British Museum these days, armed to the teeth with clipboards and notepads, I realize that they are far better informed than ever I was, growing up in the midst of it all. We visited the Pyramids and the Sphinx at least every couple of weeks, but the purpose of this, so far as I was concerned, was not to pay attention to antiquity but to have a donkey-ride and – essential, this – be allowed to choose my own donkey from the array on offer alongside the approach road to the Great Pyramid. This was effectively a taxi rank, but without any such niceties as taking the front donkey in the line. It was, rather, a process of jostling negotiation with all the donkey men in competition, and the donkeys tricked out in seductive finery – tassels, braided harness, upholstered saddles, strings of beads; brilliant in scarlet, orange, cerise, purple, turquoise. The criterion of selection, for me, was a combination of splendour of décor and the quality of the donkey itself. You were looking for as much as possible by way of tassels and beads and braiding and so forth, along with compelling personal charm. Small was preferable, dark brown fur best of all, and facial features significant – long silky eyelashes, velvet muzzle. I would spin out the process of choice for as long as possible, patrolling the line like some connoisseur of horseflesh at a bloodstock sale. The donkeys were all called Chocolate, Whisky-and-Soda or Telephone. There was a camel line also, but I was not interested in camels. Too high, and they lurched alarmingly as they rose and made those terrible groaning noises.

It was all going on, last time I went back, very much

the same – the donkey lines, the trappings, the beseech-
ing drivers. There they all were. But the lustre was
gone. I saw a line of dressed-up donkeys, and turned
soberly to the Pyramids.

Then, the Pyramids were neither here nor there. I had
grown up with Pyramids. A Pyramid was a Pyramid.
There they were, rearing starkly against the sky, dotted
with tiny climbing figures. There was a certain interest
attached to the climbers. Just possibly you might see one
of them fall off, and the various methods of ascent were
worth watching, with most climbers attended by a couple
of hired guides one of whom pulled from above while the
other heaved in the rear, their galabiyas flapping in the
wind. Each limestone block was several feet high; only the
extremely athletic could cope without some assistance. But
the pyramids themselves, as structures, were simply a part
of the known and accepted world. When I first saw the
Pyramids as an adult, I saw a preconception – they carried
now a freight of association and knowledge, they re-
sounded of the Napoleonic expedition, and Flaubert (who
climbed the Great Pyramid), and imprecise but dizzying
facts and figures about bulk and construction. They could
no longer be seen as themselves, but only through the
prism of all that went with them. And the climbing figures
had gone, which seemed somehow appropriate, along
with the irretrievable allure of the donkey lines.

The Pyramids were the backcloth to the donkey lines
and also to Mena House Hotel, where you had lemonade
and ice-creams. Mena House survives, kitted out for the

late twentieth century with a new extension but retaining its original building, a bizarre architectural combination of Moorish with stockbroker Tudor. Then, it implied a dazzling stylishness with the prospect of a stupefyingly good tea. We had lunch at Mena House on that first return visit to Egypt. It seemed to me no longer stylish but wonderfully odd, its original architecture a confection of ill-assorted influences which now looked a lot braver and more sprightly than the modern extension slapped down alongside. I saw it as a building, and the building in terms of its peculiar inspirations; the lunch was adequate but did not stupefy.

I assessed Cairo and its surroundings with the egotistic eye of childhood. What was there here for me? It is a view that is egotistic and also acquisitive, one that is in search of relevance. It ignores or discards all that is apparently of no interest, and homes in upon anything worth having. And what is worth having ranges from the luxurious choice of a donkey through such immediate and obvious targets as a memorable tea to those sights and sounds and smells which are for some indefinable reason of personal significance. What remains of it all, now, are those points of personal reference: my private map of the place.

At either side of the bridge over the river there are big trees. And to these trees, in the evenings, come the white egrets. They come in great wavering flocks, arriving out of the apricot sky in drifting skeins until the trees are studded all over with white, as though they had suddenly burst into bloom. And under the trees is a pungent compost of droppings. You can smell it from halfway across the bridge.

And I can still smell it, in a curious subliminal way. I could not describe the smell, but it is somehow there in the head – the shadow of a smell. And I know too that the egrets were the Little Egret, which stalked the fields of the cultivation all day. It would have been from there that they came flocking back each evening to these roosts. But the bridge I cannot identify. Zamalek Bridge? Bulaq Bridge? The English Bridge? Khedive Ismail Bridge? All those names are familiar, a part of the litany of the place, and all are on the maps of Cairo in the 1930s though most are gone now, swept away in deference to the universal insistence that the major landmarks of a city must reflect its recent history: 26th July Bridge now, and El Tahrir Bridge. It will be all the same to the egrets, that's for sure, if their roosts haven't been swept away too.

It is that litany of names which haunts me still. Gezira. Zamalek. Qasr el Nil. Qasr el Aini. El Ezbekiya. Ibn Tulun. The Beit el Kritiliya. But there is something awry, seeing these words in print. And what is awry, I realize, is that they should be in cold print at all. They were sounds, not sequences of letters on a page. I knew them before I could read, or write, and knew them thus in the way that children first know words – as recognizable sounds surfacing from the babble which bombards them. And because for more than fifty years these particular words have lain dormant in my head, I can hear them again now with that inner ear – as pure language floating free of the complications of writing or of spelling. To see them on the page is a shock.

On that first return to Egypt, as an adult, other dormant words floated to the surface. Arabic words and phrases. I would find that somehow I knew what an apricot tree was called. A *mish-mish*. And an accompanying phrase rose to the lips: '*Bukra fil mish-mish*,' which means roughly, 'Tomorrow never comes.' The sort of thing, perhaps, that Abdul and Hassan said, on the kitchen steps. '*Maalesh*,' I found myself saying – never mind. And a dozen other homely utterances that came swarming up, things I didn't know I knew. Once, I must have had a smattering of Arabic. An odd feeling – again as though you tapped in to some inaccessible bank of information. I have never undergone psychoanalysis, but I imagine that in a more disconcerting way that is similar: the discovery of concealed experience.

My Cairo of then is thus a landscape that is highly selective, entirely personal and only tenuously connected either to the reality of the time or the city that has overtaken both today. Indeed, there is almost nothing left of it, now. The lions on El Tahrir Bridge (Khedive Ismail, back then). Cairo Museum. The Mosque of Ibn Tulun. The Beit el Kritiliya. The zoo. But gone entirely is almost everything that gave it the flavour that remains most powerfully with me. The lines of white houseboats moored to the banks of the Nile – restaurants and cafés and places in which people lived – and the constant passage of feluccas gliding up and down, with those swooping sails. The river is almost empty, now. The ubiquitous traffic tangle of trams and gharries and carts and army trucks and a few cars. No tangle today, but a ceaseless crawl of cars, trucks, lorries, buses without even the intervention of traffic-lights or pedestrian cross-ings – the most daunting urban traffic I have seen anywhere. The elegant complicated façades of nineteenth-century mansion blocks, and the shady tree-lined pavements. Swept away, for the most part, and replaced by functional concrete.

The zoo survives, which once was a focal point of my life.

It is always appallingly hot in the lion house, and there is that rank smell which is like nothing else. The animals slink to and fro, and a keeper in the zoo uniform of tattered dark-blue cotton sweater and khaki drill shorts pushes hunks of meat through the bars with a sort of gigantic toasting fork. Favoured children (whose parents have slipped him five piastres) are allowed to climb over the barrier and help him do this. Not me, thank you – even if there are lion or tiger cubs on offer.

Once, by myself in the farthest limits of the garden at Bulaq Dakhrur in the dusk, I thought I smelled it, that unmistakable smell. My hair stood on end; I froze to the spot. There haven't been lions in Egypt for hundreds of years. I know that. They are always telling me that. But there are cobras, aren't there? And jackals. And rumours of hyenas. Why not a solitary lion holding out right here in our garden? I belt towards the house, given wings by primeval terror.

Plenty of lions in Egypt once, of course. Desert lions, living off the gazelle and antelope and ibex. Herodotus talks about them, and there they are in abundance on tomb wall-paintings, being hunted by Pharaohs. I may well have seen such representations, in the museum or at Saqqara, and formed my own views about surviving fauna, according to my own imperfect concept of time. After all, there was much other wildlife in those paintings which you could still see on all sides. Ducks and egrets and ibis and indeed the occasional gazelle, even, in the desert.

And, of course, the lion is an atavistic image. I can still experience lucid dreams of pursuit by lions, and wake up with thumping heart. An analyst would of course raise a knowing eyebrow at this. All right. And maybe a lion is also a lion, in the wilds of the subconscious, for those of us raised on the fringes of Africa.

The senior elephant patrols the footpaths, escorted by his keeper. You are invited to offer the elephant a screw of paper in which you have wrapped a few peanuts and a five-piastre piece. The elephant takes the screw of paper from your outstretched palm – the feeling is both alien and oddly intimate, warm and hairy and deft – doubles back its trunk in a salaam and then hands the screw of paper to the keeper, who unwraps it, pockets the five piastres and allows the elephant to eat the peanuts, after which it salaams once more.

The hippos float in a small lake. Summoned by their keeper, they approach the shallows, molten mud streaming from their backs, and they open pink maws edged with craggy brown teeth. For a few more piastres you can buy a scoop of potatoes from the keeper which you then hurl into the gaping mouths. This is great sport – a test of aim but also a matter of trying to target the small hippos – females and infants – who get shouldered aside by the dominant males. When sated, the hippos shut up shop – you hear a great scrunch as their jaws close – and slide away down into the water until there is nothing visible but nostrils and an oval of glistening snout.

A zoo that was heavily into visitor-participation. Or was it simply that the keepers had devised a system to supplement inadequate wages? I fed the hippos at Cairo Zoo again, a few years ago, but this was a shameless set-up by a film unit who were making a film about the history of the British Council, which began life in Egypt in the 1920s. I'm not at all sure how or where this episode was to be slotted into the sequence of British Council activities, or if it ever was, but the shoot took place, with much commotion of a Land Rover cavalcade of cameramen and equipment into the traffic-prohibited paths of the zoo. The hippos had been deprived of their breakfasts so that they should be properly receptive, and I duly pitched potatoes at them. The lake was not a lake at all, but a large pond, and the hippos too were half the size that I remembered.

The lions, the hippos, that elephant were part of an accumulated familiarity, along with the entire backcloth of the city – a rich continuous clamour of people and places, shot with the vivid detail of intimacy. The Gezira Sporting Club, with the intoxicating expanse of a real, chlorine-reeking, blue-tiled swimming-pool, and green swards of grass with blinding white fences, and a babble of English voices. Groppi's, where you had tea and cakes in a garden covered with a vine-hung pergola and set out with marble-topped tables and precarious iron chairs. The array of patisserie was as sumptuous and ornate as a jeweller's window, and I would be driven frantic by the constrictions of choice – two, and two only. So which? The boat-shaped ones with the rich cream filling? The ones topped with sugar-dusted chocolate logs? The brimming éclairs? And then there was Lappas the grocer, where sugar, tea, coffee, raisins were measured into midnight-blue bags and closed with a twirl. And Cicurel, the department store where Lucy bought the lengths of material out of which she made my clothes, and the ribbons with which my hair was tied. I resented having to wear a hair-ribbon, but was entranced by the lavish choice – silk, satin, velvet, ribbed, embroidered – as tantalizing to the eye as Groppi cakes were to the tongue.

And then there is that other kind of intimacy, when suddenly the place is hitched to something more immediate, to the echo of emotion.

Lucy and I walk beside the Nile. She will not speak to me. I have done something wrong, something appalling. Lucy is tight-lipped and silent. She has said that she is going to leave. She is going to pack her bags and leave. She will tell my mother when we get home. I am filled with cold fear. I believe her, utterly. I trot alongside, pleading. I am sorry, I weep. I am sorry, sorry, sorry. But she is implacable. I trail behind her now, no longer able even to weep, with a hard, tight knot of fear in my stomach. The white sails of the feluccas on the river swoop against the brown water. My feet crunch on the fallen leaves of eucalyptus. Cairo shouts and clatters around us. Everything is quite normal, but steeped in unreality. I walk in a daze of horror, and of guilt. You've no one to thank but yourself, says Lucy.

I can retrieve that emotion quite clearly. The horror, the desolation of abandonment. Goodness knows what I had done. In fact, Lucy threatened to pack her bags quite frequently, but this occasion must have been of a different order. And I see now what lies beyond it, why it is so potent. I see what it is about – the insecurity of children brought up by those who are not their parents.

And I see too that Lucy was wrong to trade on this, however fearful my transgression. She knew that she wasn't really going to leave; I did not. In truth she was devoted to me and had she left the precipitating factor would not have been my behaviour but her ambivalent relationship with my mother. But children who are thus cared for know deep in their beings that something is out of order. Parents do not walk out; others can and do. And so far as I was concerned Lucy was the centre of everything. My parents were peripheral. Walking beside the Nile that day, clenched in anguish, I never gave them a thought.

Children do not contemplate an alternative to the status quo. It never occurred to me that it might be a more natural arrangement if my mother looked after me. In fact, the idea if proposed would have been appalling. The only threat to security was that Lucy should not be there. Unthinkable, and terrifying. And for the most part it was unthought. Lucy was there, day in and day out, and throughout my hoarded vision of Cairo she is always at my side, sometimes sharply so, sometimes just as a cloudy, reassuring presence.

I am confronted by a glass case in which there is the stuffed form of a Nile catfish of great size – a vast grey creature with cascading whiskers, displayed against a setting of weed and gravel. I am mesmerized. I do not want to go on looking at this thing, but I have to. I know that it is going to haunt me, but I cannot tear myself away. Come along, says Lucy, somewhere above and beyond. I stand there, shuddering.

Where can this have been? A museum, an aquarium? The sight is quite detached now from any setting. But it did indeed pursue me. The river, thereafter, was tainted – a place of secret horrors. I studied its grey-brown surface uneasily for a glimpse of the sinister shapes that lurked below. Could they perhaps crawl out, in the dusk? The evening walks along the Gezira corniche became less enticing. Years later, I read *Beowulf* and recognized Grendel's mere immediately – that alliance of water and monstrosity. Of course, the Nile.

We are in Ezbekiya Gardens, on a bench. Lucy is knitting. We have brought a picnic tea. Tomato sandwiches, and a Thermos. Babies in prams parade before us on the gravelled paths, and courting couples, and children with skipping-ropes. 'Don't wave that sandwich around like that,' scolds Lucy. High above us in the hard blue sky there float the city's scavenging kites. The kites have perfect vision; they can home in on anything, and plummet down. Lucy knows of a child who had her finger taken off, along with her sandwich. I tuck the sandwich in a fold of my dress, and foil the kites.

We are at the Beit el Kritiliya, for which I have a passion. I would rather go there than anywhere: the Club, Ezbekiya Gardens, the Citadel. Groppi's even.

The place fascinates me – the suggestion of strange, alternative lives. The couches covered with opulent, velvet-textured rugs. The vine-hung terraces on to which you emerge and see, below and around, the teeming hidden Cairo roof-life. And above all the secretive lattice-work windows overhanging the narrow street, from which you can see but not be seen. I want to go and live in the Beit el Kritiliya. I tell myself stories in which I do precisely that.

The Beit el Kritiliya was, and is, one of the few surviving domestic buildings of the Mameluke period. It is in fact two interconnected buildings of the sixteenth and seventeenth centuries, alongside the entrance to Ibn Tulun Mosque. They had been rescued from dereliction by the Committee for the Preservation of Arab Monuments which had then allowed Major Gayer-Anderson Pasha to live there, restore the houses in 1935 and use them for the display of his own collection of oriental furnishings. Gayer-Anderson had lived in Egypt since 1907, first on secondment to the Egyptian army and later as Oriental Secretary to the British Residency. He was a fervent collector and the Beit el Kritiliya, now known as the Gayer-Anderson Museum, still houses the bulk of his collection, which he left to the Egyptian government. But a crucial item found its way to the British Museum: the Gayer-Anderson cat, a superb black basalt statuette with a gold ring through its nose which lives in the Egyptian Hall. I pay it a ceremonial visit once a year or so. Gayer-Anderson had been a close friend of my paternal grandmother and indeed family folklore had it that the cat had been loaned to her before being donated to the British Museum and stood for a while in the centre of the dining-room table in her house in Harley Street.

When I went to the Beit el Kritiliya on my first return to Egypt I could barely recover at all that mystique it once held. The windows I found so intriguing were of course the *mashrabiya* windows which are the most prominent feature of the architecture of that period and beyond – carved screens which surround tiny galleries projecting into the street and enabling the harem dwellers within both to enjoy any cool breezes going and oversee the street life below. They are delicately ornate, as well as being functional, and it is thus that I see them now, but without that intoxicating quality that I can only just recover. But every now and then it did come smoking up, as I toured the museum – a whiff of it from an alcove lined with Turkish rugs, another gust from the courtyard, from the roof-garden, from the floor-tiles. And there on a wall amid a clutter of oddly assorted pictures was a drawing by my grandmother, who was quite a good amateur artist, of my aunt Margaret – a further eerie personal resonance.

My childhood reaction to the Beit el Kritiliya smacks of romantic orientalism, it now seems to me. This would have been inspired by the *Arabian Nights* – I owned the Andrew Lang version, with line drawings of trousered and turbaned figures, and girls in diaphanous garments. Courtyards, fountains, and no doubt the occasional glimpse of a *mashrabiya* window. I must have seen the Beit el Kritiliya not as fact but as fiction made manifest – a marvellous concrete version of my own entrenched habit of internal fantasy. For a while, I plunged into a long-running private fiction in which the action of the *Arabian Nights* was carried out in the Beit el Kritiliya, with me starring as everybody.

I note now that this was an entirely literary vision of the orient. It did not occur to me at the time that it had any relevance to the real Middle East in which we lived – as indeed it did not. I saw a fascinating confirmation of the emotive power of stories. These things were so potent that they could come to life, just as I had always suspected. But to visit the Beit el Kritiliya as an adult was to find that the *Arabian Nights* had been relegated to a decorative mythology – and quite right too, I suppose. There indeed were lamps of the kind that you rub to summon up a genie. There was a scimitar. There was a fountain. But they were lamps and scimitars and fountains, not hallucinations. Now, my concern was to try to sort out the complexities of the post-medieval history of Egypt, and the tangled sequence of the construction of Cairo.

Several Cairos, in fact. The first city of all was Heliopolis – pharaonic, Greek, destroyed by the Persians and surviving today only as a sprawling suburb of modern Cairo. A centre of scholarship, once, known to Herodotus and to Plato – quite extinguished except for its name. It was succeeded by Babylon, where the Romans built a fort which survives on the extreme southern side of the modern city. This was Christian Coptic Cairo, and there was also a synagogue from which there exist still parts of the ancient Torah, dispersed around the great libraries of the world. Babylon was captured in the Arab invasion of the seventh century, but its huddled defensive site did not suit the Arabs and now, at the beginning of the Muslim period, Cairo moved again.

Fustat, just to the north of Babylon, was Muslim Cairo from then until it was burned down in the twelfth century. Today it is nothing but a fuming rubbish heap patrolled by pi-dogs where the intrepid visitor can still find a harvest of Islamic potsherds. I have a treasured fragment given me by a friend – a piece a few inches across which was the base of a shallow dish on which two little black fish leap against a background of creamy glaze. Fustat was burned down by its own ruler in an attempt to persuade the inhabitants to move into the newer city to the north, el Qahira, which could more easily be defended against attackers, and the only buildings left standing were the mosques of Amr Ibn el 'As and Ibn Tulun. Cairo took another step to the north, and arrived now at what is still the old city – the dense and cluttered quadrangle between the two ancient gates of Bab Zuwayla and Bab el Nasr. This was medieval Cairo, the Cairo of the Fatimids and then the Mamelukes, of which the basic structure at least remains, along with mosques and sections of the original encircling wall. Every contemporary tourist visits Khan el Khalili, which has been a bazaar since 1400.

The Citadel broods above the city on a spur of the Muqattam Hills. Saladin built it towards the end of the twelfth century, and at the beginning of the nineteenth Mohammed Ali, the Albanian soldier who effectively ruled Egypt on behalf of the Turkish Porte for over forty years, trapped five hundred Mamelukes in it and slaughtered them. Mohammed Ali created European Cairo, in the sense that it was he who invited and encouraged European interest, especially French. There now began that accelerating expansion of the city which was to produce the dizzying population leaps of the nineteenth and twentieth centuries – from a quarter of a million to nearly 600,000 between the Napoleonic census and the end of the century, over 2 million by 1947, 4 million in 1966, 14 million today. European Cairo was the Cairo of the boulevards and the Frenchified mansion blocks, of Garden City and Zamalek, but the invasion of European capital and investment was also the prompt for the galloping expansion of the city and the process whereby the overwhelming dominance of an agricultural society was to cease. By the end of the twentieth century there would be almost as many urban-dwelling Egyptians as fellaheen.

It was European Cairo that I knew, for the most part, with the occasional emotive taste of something else: the Beit el Kritiliya, the City of the Dead, the Citadel. I knew nothing of sequential Cairo, but sensed in some way, I believe, a palimpsest. It was clear that Cairo – all of Egypt, indeed – was a disorderly place in more senses than one. It was a place of cultural confusion – I was battered throughout my childhood with nationalities and allegiances. British, French, Greek, Syrian, Lebanese, Turkish. Church of England, Muslim, Coptic, Jewish. All different, in significant but unstated ways. I placed them within the only context that a child has available – the personal context – and sorted them out into some kind of order. British was us, and most of the people we knew well. Egyptian was the world at large, the myriad faces of the city, of the cultivation. French was the scented, chauffeur-driven mother of a wealthy family we sometimes visited, who spoke with an interesting accent and kissed my mother on both cheeks. Less appealingly, French was also Mademoiselle, who gave me French lessons in Alexandria. I revelled in *Les Malheurs de Sophie* but hated Mademoiselle, who had bad breath and corsets that faintly creaked as she moved. Lucy connived in my dislike, feeling her territory threatened.

Greek was the lady in the grocery near the villa we had one summer in Alexandria, a black-clad mountain topped with a beaming face and liquid dark kindly eyes, who gave me sweets in a twist of paper. And the girl behind the ribbon counter at Cicurel, who tipped Lucy off when there had been a delivery of interesting new stock, and who had the same fathomless eyes. Lebanese was those mysterious daughters of Nunn's, and Syrian was the nurse with a cloud of dark hair who looked after the children of friends of my parents, and whose methods sent Lucy into a frenzy of pursed lips and muttered asides. Turkish was Turkish Delight and the big carpet in the drawing-room. Church of England was the cathedral where we went for the Christmas carol service and christenings of other people's babies and where I had apparently been christened myself. Muslim was the minarets and the muezzin's call and the gardeners upended at their prayers in a shady bit of the garden and Ramadan when nobody could eat till evening, which made them irritable and volatile and so required tact and forbearance.

Coptic was mysterious. Coptic had an aura which I could not identify but of which I was definitely conscious. And this I now realize is where in some random and maverick way I homed in unknowing upon the chronology of the country. Here and there, over the months and years, as I grew up, aspects of the place meshed crucially and unforgettably with my own life. I didn't know what it was I saw or heard or failed to understand, but I never forgot.

Every Christmas there was a carol service at the cathedral which was known as the Toy Service. The point of it was that all attending children should donate a toy, which would be given to the families of poor Copts. You carried your toy up the aisle, at the end of the service, and deposited it on a pile at the feet of the benignly smiling bishop while the congregation crooned carols. You were done up to the nines for the occasion – party frock, white socks, Cicurel hair-ribbon. I loathed and detested the whole event, on account of the party frock and the socks, and because I couldn't sing, and most of all because of the toy donation. You could not give any old toy; it had to be something you were especially fond of. I argued passionately over this. Why? What difference could it possibly make to the poor Coptic children whether it was a favourite toy or not? Why could I not give them the doll given me by a visitor which was brand-new, had real hair, eyes that shut and a pink net dress but about which I was unenthusiastic? Lucy was implacable. It was the element of sacrifice that mattered. And so, every year I stumped sullenly up the aisle clutching some beloved hairless teddy, or wall-eyed doll. I like to think that my present agnosticism is the product of informed and intelligent reflection, but I suspect that the seeds may have been sown back then, when I was coerced annually into irrational sacrifice to the strains of 'Away in a Manger'.

But what reached me also, over and beyond all the negative elements of the Toy Service, was the specialness of Copts. Copt meant good. Copt meant élite, in some mysterious way. I must have realized that Copts were Christians, as I was supposed to be myself. But there was more to it than that, and I now realize that the further element was the respect accorded to the Coptic community as the only surviving element of pre-Islamic Egypt, the oldest Egyptians of all, the descendants of the Egypt of Rome, of Greece, of the Pharaohs. There was undoubtedly a doctrinal element in this respect, as enshrined in the Toy Service and vague admonitions of Lucy's. But Lucy knew little of and was not interested in the Egyptian past. There was some further way in which the Copts were distinguished, nothing to do with being Christian; this seeped through to me, and I can now identify it. It was the sanctity of ancestry.

And, in the same way, I recognized other things as phenomenal but inexplicable. The wall-paintings in the tombs at Saqqara, which showed scenes that were exotic and yet familiar: strangely clad figures, but also the birds and animals and plants of the Nile landscape that I knew. The great mosques – Ibn Tulun and Sultan Hassan. The Beit el Kritiliya. The Citadel. Each in turn served as a backdrop for my own self-absorbed existence, but was also in some way impenetrable, teasing and enticing. And this surely was an effect of the process whereby children learn to perceive the restrictions of their state. They are self-absorbed, and confined by their self-absorption as well as by the obvious fetter of ignorance, but there are sudden chinks in the self-absorption, and sudden glimpses of the very nature of ignorance.

There is one final and apt occasion in my head when the continuities of the place were fused with what was happening to me, and with what I felt and understood.

I have been taken out for the afternoon by a friend of my father's, a man I have never met before, who has come from Khartoum, where my father is now working. He has taken me to the museum. We look at the things from Tutankhamun's tomb. He explains them to me, in a grown-up way, as though I were older than I am. I stand looking at the great gold mask, at the chariot, at the sarcophagus, and am filled with a confused solemnity. Lucy is not with us. I am alone with this stranger whose name and face have subsequently faded away but who hangs over the afternoon as a kindly presence, concerned about me in a way that I cannot identify. I sense his concern, and the fact that I am spotlit in some way, affected as though ill, and that this man is like a doctor, perturbed about an ailment of which I do not feel the symptoms.

Lucy is not with us because my parents are getting divorced, and this is the afternoon of the court hearing, at which her presence is required. All this has been explained to me, partly by Lucy and partly by my mother. I know too that Lucy and I are going soon to England, for ever, and that I will live first with my grandmothers – going from one to the other – and then later with my father, when he comes from Khartoum.

I know all this, but passively. I do not know what to do with these facts. They hang above the glass cases in the museum, above the mask, above the jewellery, which are more immediate. I know only that things are out of the ordinary, and that I feel solemn, and vaguely important.

I was eleven. Lucy had to be at the court hearing to give

evidence as to my mother's adultery. My mother had been living for some while with a man she had met a year or so before – an army officer – and my father had agreed to a divorce. He would be granted custody of me, which my mother had not requested. Lucy would take me back to England, where my father would find us a home and me a boarding school as soon as he could wind up his affairs in the Sudan.

Back then, divorce was not the commonplace happening that it is today. It carried a stigma. I had heard the word – as one uttered by grown-ups in a particular tone, a mysteriously loaded word. Lucy and I had been living for some while cheek by jowl with my mother's new domestic arrangements, and were offended by them. Our reaction had been to withdraw into our private enclave. We tried to ignore my mother and her companion, and they steered clear of us.

Thinking about it all now, I see that I was in a sense cushioned from the effect of divorce by the distance that there had always been between my mother and myself. The fact that she was now, in effect, discarding me along with my father was not as shattering as it would be for a child for whom a mother is the crucial figure. I would still have Lucy, who was far more important to me. It would be Lucy who would take me to England. It never occurred to me that I would have to lose Lucy also, eventually. And in the event I was not to see my mother again for two years, after we left Egypt, by which time I was someone else.

I do not know who the kindly friend of my father's

was who took me to the museum that day, but my father subsequently wrote to Lucy that he had reported of that afternoon that I was charming and very nicely behaved. I was much gratified by this; nobody had ever said such a thing before. And when, years later, I saw the Tutankhamun treasures again, the immediacies were reversed: the mask and the chariot sank away and the portentous atmosphere of that afternoon came flooding back.

Chapter Five

I did not go to school in Egypt. I could have done – there were English schools, but they were in Cairo so there would have been a problem about transport. For whatever reason, school was never proposed and at some point, without fuss, Lucy turned herself from nurse into governess. This now seems to me a bold and indeed valiant move. I don't think that she herself had had much, if any, secondary education. She wrote an exemplary copperplate hand, was competent with figures and a keen reader, but that was about it. What she did was to discover the organization which exactly catered for those in our situation. Possibly my parents had a hand in it, but my feeling is that they did not. I don't remember either of them being involved or indeed taking a great deal of interest in my lessons. It was Lucy, all the way, and the organization upon which she lit was the Parents National Educational Union – the PNEU.

The PNEU was, and still is, both a system and a philosophy of education. It ran schools in England, but it also offered a sort of do-it-yourself education kit to expatriate parents. The child was signed up with the

PNEU centre, and then the timetables, the books and expansive instructions on how to administer them were dispatched at intervals. I have some of this material in front of me now – Form III (A & B), ages 11 to 18. Pupil's name: Penelope (IIIB). April 1944. I was just eleven, so evidently we were keeping up nicely. The PNEU's credo is magisterial: 'Children are born persons. They are not born either good or bad, but with possibilities for good and for evil. The principles of authority on the one hand, and of obedience on the other, are natural, necessary and fundamental . . .' Straight Rousseau – and it continues along the same lines.

The PNEU motto is 'Education is an atmosphere, a discipline, and a life' . . . We hold that the child's mind is no mere sack to hold ideas; but is rather, if the figure may be allowed, a spiritual organism, with an appetite for all knowledge . . . children should be taught, as they become mature enough to understand such teaching, that the chief responsibility which rests on them as persons is the acceptance or rejection of ideas.

All very high-minded. Reading it now, I wouldn't quarrel with many of the sentiments, even if the language seems a touch sententious. The philosophical synopsis continues by outlining the system which was the cornerstone of the PNEU method – the telling-back process.

As knowledge is not assimilated until it is reproduced, children should 'tell back' after a single reading or hearing: or should write on some part of what they have read. A single reading is insisted on, because children have naturally a great power of attention; but this force is dissipated by the rereading of passages, and also, by questioning, summarizing, and the like.

Lucy read: I told back and, when older, wrote back. I see now what a luxurious educational process it was. Short on expertise, perhaps, but rich in that crucial element – one-to-one attention. Lucy may have been under-qualified, but I had all of her, every day. Together we applied ourselves to the requirements of the PNEU.

The timetable astonishes me. It is chopped up into twenty-minute periods (ah – that natural power of attention . . .) and covered the mornings only, six days a week. Formal teaching was a half-day process, then. Probably the idea was that the afternoons would be devoted to sport or organized games, also high on the PNEU agenda; in our case, needless to say, this went by the board. In the afternoons I played in the garden while Lucy sat under a tree and knitted. Or, on star occasions, we went into Cairo. The timetable begins each day with Old Testament or New Testament, except for Wednesdays, which shot off at a tangent into Natural History. Even now I find that Wednesday has a slightly raffish feel. Fridays began with Picture Study. The PNEU sent coloured reproductions of famous pictures, two or three per term, and we studied them. I remember an interior by Jan Steen, and a Romney portrait, and a Gainsborough. Picture Study had us baffled, I'm afraid.

Neither Lucy nor I knew quite what we were supposed to do. Eventually, having studied the Jan Steen and the rest into the ground we tacitly agreed to turn Friday into a reading period.

We read the Bible from end to end. Well, not quite. Lucy had her own ideas about what was appropriate so we skipped Leviticus and Numbers and Chronicles and indeed much of the Old Testament. Formally, at any rate – but I certainly dipped into it on my own, partly in search of that stuff about issues of blood and nakedness that had Lucy running for cover, but also because I liked all those catalogues of names, those sonorous injunctions, that language. When I look at the King James Version now it is resonantly familiar. Those rhythms and cadences are ingrained somewhere deep within me. By the time I was in my early twenties I knew that I was an agnostic, which presumably – and ironically – stemmed at least in part from that early emphasis in training for responsibility in the acceptance or rejection of ideas. Intensive exposure to the King James Version did not make me a Christian, but it gave me a grounding in the English language for which I am profoundly grateful. And when I see the pallid replacements favoured by the Church of England today – the New International Bible and the deplorable Good News Bible – I am amazed, and saddened.

Arithmetic featured strongly in the timetable. Every day, except when Geometry was suggested as an alternative. This was a tricky area. We had the books, which supplied the problems and indeed the answers at the back, but they were short on explanation. Sooner or later we reached the summit of Lucy's own education in basic mathematics, and after that we were on our own. It was a question of grimly working through the syllabus, page by page, and hoping that I would get the answers to the exercises right because if I hadn't then we would have to set to and find out why, which could be a taxing process. Geometry had a certain appeal because of the technical grandeur of the projector and the compasses, but we were floundering, and knew it. And I remember that eventually Algebra appeared, and had us well and truly floored from the word go. Guiltily, we abandoned it and settled for an overkill of long division, which I could manage.

Friday, third period: Plutarch's *Lives*. Surely not? But even as I look askance at this item on the timetable there floats into the head a vestigial memory. A small green book. Stories in it. No pictures. A reaction that seems neutral, which is perhaps why the only identifying detail is the colour of the book. Evidently I was not seized by Plutarch's *Lives*. And indeed I can see why, having looked at Plutarch recently, for quite other reasons. Unless this small green digest had managed somehow to enliven those stern narratives it is hard to see how they would grab an eleven-year-old. A curious choice on the part of the PNEU.

Citizenship, equally so. Wednesdays, straight after the lush indulgence of Natural History. But I remember

Citizenship very well. Again, for negative reasons. If we were leery about Geometry and Algebra, Citizenship had us completely fazed. There was once more the accompanying book. But its prose was impenetrable and it talked of things neither of us could follow at all. It was dealing I think with the history of Parliament – certainly there was a picture of Big Ben somewhere. No doubt it was a supportive text to *Our Island Story*, that defiant patriotic tract, but where *Our Island Story* was all sound and fury, the citizenship book plunged into a morass of allusion, and brandished words we did not understand. We had to keep reaching for the dictionary. There was a chapter about something called a Witan. Even the dictionary abandoned us here. Years later, I had to write an essay at university about Anglo-Saxon government, and there again was the Witan. For an instant, I was back in the nursery at Bulaq Dakhrur, glowering at that uncooperative book. Which we presently consigned to the bottom of my desk, in another of those tacit acts of collusion.

Repetition, every day. Repetition: Poem. Repetition: Bible. Repetition: Week's Work. Learning by heart, we called it. I could still, if required, declaim a good deal of the beginning of Macaulay's *Lays of Ancient Rome*, and, back then, did so constantly. While pelting up and down the drive on my bike, or to enliven the after-lunch rest time, lying on my bed in vest and knickers: 'Lars Porsena of Clusium, by the nine gods he swore . . .' And chunks of Genesis and tracts of the Psalms and the whole of St Paul's Epistle to the Corinthians, Chapter 13. And arbitrary swathes of poetry: 'Swiftly walk o'er the western wave, Spirit of Night! . . .' 'Abou ben Adam (may his tribe increase!) . . .' James Elroy Flecker. Rupert Brooke. Oscar Wilde, for heaven's sake. The choices were maverick and had little to do with the PNEU, I suspect, and much more with what happened to be on my parents' bookshelves because Lucy suffered from a continuous shortfall of equipment. The books were sent out from England by the PNEU, and they frequently failed to arrive, along with other rather more vital wartime supplies. So we fell back on what was available, which accounts for some of the more esoteric areas of my reading. Somerset Maugham. The plays of Noël Coward. When we ran out of the material advocated by the PNEU, we simply read anything that came to hand, rather than not read at all. And the PNEU said, 'Learn by heart' so learn by heart I did. Anything, pretty well.

I don't remember objecting in the least. Word-perfect, you had to be, and that became a matter of pride. I suppose that as a system it was an educational anachronism, but I have a soft spot for it. I relish, now, those eclectic mental furnishings, apparently indestructible.

Science featured three times only on the timetable, as Natural History, Botany and General Science. I strongly suspect now that General Science went to the bottom of the Mediterranean, because there is no accompanying vision whatsoever. But Natural History and Botany are vivid. This was our favourite area by far. The Natural History textbook was by one Arabella Buckley, and was called *Eyes and No Eyes*. It was about the flora and fauna of the English pond and stream and it had colour plates in which the different things illustrated were identified by letters – *a, b, c, d*. For some reason I was immensely struck by this scholarly touch. I revered Arabella Buckley, and pored over the text and the plates. I would then descend upon the garden ditch, armed with net and jam jar, and pursue my own scholarship. The catch was frequently disconcerting, and not at all like the inhabitants of Arabella Buckley's genteel Devon waters. Caddis fly? Water boatman? Never mind – it was science, and I was doing it.

I know now that Arabella Buckley was a real person, as it were. Not just a resonant name on the cover of a book. She was secretary to Charles Lyell, the great nineteenth-century geologist who was Darwin's patron and friend. She knew Darwin, and must have been a part of that contentious, combative and stimulating world of nineteenth-century scientific studies. I have conjured up *Eyes and No Eyes* in the British Library. It arrived in a dozen little booklets – not what I remembered at all – half of them written by someone called R. Cadwallader-Smith, a resolutely Edwardian name. Published in 1901, so the PNEU was not exactly up-to-date in its textbook recommendations. And there indeed were the colour plates with the identifying letters which had so impressed me: '*a*. dragonfly feeding. *b*. dragonfly creeping out of grub skin.' But the text no longer had the command and authority I recalled. What I read now was something entirely different – the cosily instructive tone of the late nineteenth-century children's writer. 'Croak, croak, croak, we hear the frogs in the month of March . . . The mother frogs are laying their tiny dark eggs in the water. Each egg is not bigger than a grain of sand. But it has a coat of jelly . . .' And presently the author introduces that familiar participatory child character, as though she doubted the reader's ability to stomach instruction for much longer without the reassurance of a crony with whom to identify. There is Tom the gamekeeper's son – 'a Devonshire lad' – who watches young otters, and a sanctimonious little girl called Peggy who instructs her friend Peter: 'And look, Peter, the yellow lines on the white flowers point straight to the narrow end of the flower-heart, where the insects find the honey.' Can this have been the prose which so fired me with scientific enthusiasm, and sent me off on my own researches?

It must have been, and I suspect that Arabella Buckley inspired my own first written work. I have it still. It was written in 1940, when I was seven, on the squared pages of an exercise book in much better handwriting than I have today. It is called, succinctly, *Egypt*, and on the back page it has a grandiose list of contents with chapter titles. I had run out of steam at Chapter Five: Egyptian Reptiles. The beginning of Chapter One is an excursion into rudimentary sociology:

The Fellahs children are usually of a great many, a boy is treasured much more by the parents than a girl and if a boy and a girl are sent out together the boy will always ride a donkey while the girl walks along behind. While they are still children the girls will go into black veils over their heads but undernearth [*sic*] they wear a gay dress, the women do too, but if they are married it is entirely covered by black.

The style is ponderous to a degree, but I warm to the hint of feminist outrage. At one point I got carried away with a description of the Egyptian sunset ('the clouds are transformed into a rich pink hue by the glow of the setting sun . . .') but then evidently decided this was frivolous and crossed it out, embarking on a stern paragraph about the export of cotton. Or was this an acknowledgement of stylistic catastrophe? If so, the perception did not stretch far. The weighty language persists, with what now seems to me a distinct note of nineteenth-century didacticism – pages and pages about the Egyptian crow and the date palm and the horned viper. The shadow of Arabella Buckley, for sure.

Or possibly Bentham and Hooker, the treatise which was Lucy's prized possession and with which we did Botany and tried to identify the few wild flowers which grew on the fringes of the fields. Scarlet pimpernel, shepherd's purse, vetch. Matching up quite nicely with the text and illustrations in Bentham and Hooker. We made lists of what we had found, and I tried to reflect the professionalism of Arabella Buckley and Messrs Bentham and Hooker by making my own line-drawings in pen and India ink. Not a success. I had no artistic talent. There in my head was the aspiration, and there on the page the ugly botched reality, irrevocably separated by frustration and despair. Why could I not produce those precise, allusive lines? Even Lucy, who had no artistic training, could manage a passable sketch of a plant. I can recover still that exasperated sense of being in some way crippled, and I think it was not to do with being unable to draw, but a temporary rage with the condition of childhood. Every now and then, children identify themselves. They see what they are – people at an early stage of development, with all that that implies. And the perception is appalling.

I couldn't draw, but Lucy had done a good job on my handwriting. That would have been the hours of pothooks which by the time I achieved Form III (A) had become Dictation and Writing. Much copying out of chosen passages took place. In the period called English Grammar we dismantled sentences and put the spare parts into columns labelled Nouns, Verbs, Adjectives and so forth. This was good fun. But there was also a period called Analysis and Parsing, which still gives Thursdays an ominous ring. Again, dissection was involved – that much we understood. But here Lucy was out of her depth, and together we thrashed about amid subjects and objects and subordinate clauses and prepositions. I would unravel a piece of prose and try to find the appropriate category for each component part – and always there were rogue elements, words and phrases that jeeringly refused to be corralled. Lucy read and reread the manual, and I would watch anxiously with an odd and uncomfortable emotion which I now recognize as compunction. It was because of me that she was being put through this. I hope and think that eventually we decided I could get through life quite satisfactorily without Analysis and Parsing, as indeed I have.

Geography meant Bartholomew's Atlas, of course, and the global rash of pink. Latin we played about with, insincerely. *Mensa. Puella. Amo, amas, amat.* Lucy did not take Latin seriously, and her contempt spilled over to me. I was still having trouble with Latin at eighteen, confronted with Oxford Prelims. For French we enjoyed ourselves with the Père Castor story books, and another series about a splendid bourgeois rodent called Madame Souris, who went shopping and nagged her husband and batted her children around. There was also *Perlette: l'histoire d'une goutte d'eau*, a wonderfully surreal tale about a drop of rain which falls into a stream and ends up in the ocean. The amorphous areas of Literature and Composition we simply included in the great untrammelled indulgence of Reading.

For Reading was what we were best at, and we knew it. We were happy to read till the cows came home, and did so. Lucy read; I read. I told back; I wrote back. We read everything the PNEU suggested – Greek and Roman mythology, Norse mythology, stories from Chaucer and *Piers Plowman*, the *Arabian Nights*. And then we read it all again and when we were saturated in it we

turned to whatever else we could find. *Nicholas Nickleby.*
The Talisman. The Rose and the Ring. Mary Webb, who
was responsible for a concept of rural English society
that was to cause me much perplexity when eventually I
arrived at my grandmother's home in Somerset after the
war. Some of this reading would have been shared with
Lucy, much of it I did on my own – the compulsive
retreat of a solitary child.

I had children's books too, as such, though not a
wealth of them. *Alice, The Wind in the Willows, The Just
So Stories, The Jungle Books.* All of them read and reread
because there was no library available from which to
ring the changes. And when the Arthur Ransome books
found their way to the Express Bookshop in Cairo I
became infatuated, addicted. I saved up my pocket money
to buy them as they arrived – objects so covetable as to
be awesome, those green bindings with the gold lettering,
and the distinctive dust-jackets. I read them like some
awestruck peasant, gawping at the goings-on of these
incredible children: their airy confidence, their sophistication, their independence. The narratives patently bore no
relation to real life, but were enthralling as pure fantasy.
And then there was the matter of the ambience, this
exotic landscape of hills and lakes and greenery and rain
and boats and peculiar birds and animals. From time to
time I would lift my eyes from the page to look out at
my own humdrum environment of palms and donkeys
and camels and the hoopoe stabbing the lawn.

Greek mythology was another matter – altogether more

accessible. Here, I was without inhibitions. I could march in and make it mine, manipulate the resources to my own convenience. Of course, I was right in there anyway – Penelope – but saddled with a thoroughly unsatisfying role. All that daft weaving, and it was not even clear that she was particularly beautiful. So I would usurp other parts, wallowing in vicarious experience, hidden away in the hammock of creepers behind the swimming-pool. I would re-enact it all, amending the script, starring in every episode. I was Helen, languishing in the arms of Paris. I was Achilles, nobly dying. I was Nausicaa, nude and distinctly sexy on a beach. The erotic overtones had not escaped me – or rather, they had reached mysterious levels of my own nature. I perceived that there was something going on that I found distinctly exciting, and reacted accordingly. I ceased to be a podgy child daydreaming in a hedge, and shot up and away into a more vivid place where I controlled everything, where I was the heroine and the creator all at once, where I set the scene and furnished the dialogue and called the shots. I dressed myself in wonderful clothes, and felt the drapery slide across my adult limbs. I fled, as Daphne, sensing the wind in my hair and my own speed and then the strange insidious shiver as I began to turn into a tree. I walked the ramparts of Troy, I was rescued from the Minotaur, I listened for Orpheus. I became adept. I could slide off into this other world at will, trudging along the canal path behind Lucy, so busy in the head that I saw and heard nothing.

It cannot be done, now. Perhaps the next best thing is

writing fiction but that, alas, has not the transforming element of identification. You may create, but you do not become. Reading Greek mythology today, I get an occasional emotive whiff of lost capacity.

I believe that the experience of childhood reading is as irretrievable as any other area of childhood experience. It is extinguished by the subsequent experience of reading with detachment, with objectivity, with critical judgement. That ability to fuse with the narrative and the characters is gone. It is an ability that seems now both miraculous and enviable. And anyone who has had the temerity to write for children must be for ever reminded of it.

But children are distinctly selective in their acts of identification and their abandoned fusion with a text. Some sort of judgement is indeed exercised. Norse mythology never engaged me in the same way. All that fire and ice was off-putting, somehow. And who would want to be Brynhilde, who gave an impression of being overweight and had plaits, which were not glamorous at all, in my view. Involvement could take other forms, too. Lucy and I read *Nicholas Nickleby* together, on the pansy-strewn sofa in the nursery, taking a paragraph each, Lucy resuming sewing when it was my turn to read, both of us openly weeping at the sad bits. We exercised our objectivity and our critical capacities all right, but in the immediate sense of outrage at this display of inhumanity. We discussed exactly what we would do to the Squeers family if we got the chance. If we could take Smike in we would feed him up with Lucy's porridge and he would have the small spare room. We responded as though to an account of things happening to people we knew, with the intensity of personal involvement. The context of the book, its nineteenth-century setting, was neither here nor there. We read as literary innocents, and I realize now that there is an eerie advantage to be had in this.

I never acquired a comic, but at some point I came across cartoon strips in newspapers or magazines and was hooked but also baffled by the evident sophistication. Popeye was an especial challenge: I couldn't understand the running joke about spinach, which we did not have. And then there was Jane, the peroxide blonde with gargantuan bust and cleavage; I thought her immensely appealing but could not work out exactly why. The *New Yorker* sometimes found its way into the house and I pored over it, trying to decode the advertisements. Nylon stockings? Waffle-makers? Coca-Cola? Again, something was awry with my own language. This was English, but not an English I recognized. I saw that this rich, glib prose and these jaunty pictures reflected some complex and confident other world of which I knew nothing whatsoever, more unreachable even than the England I could barely remember but whose icons and mythologies were all around me. Pondering the teasing terminology of the *New Yorker* advertisements, I came up once more against the opaque screen of culture, and identified a difficulty over and beyond the familiar difficulties of words you did not understand. Here was a world far more inaccessible than those of Greek mythology or of *Nicholas Nickleby*.

I lived in a condition of frenzied internal narrative, all of it entirely derivative. Neither the PNEU nor Lucy had arrived at the concept of creative writing for children, so it was never suggested that I try my hand at stories. I told them to myself, instead, lifting the themes and the characters from what I had read and making personal adjustments. In time, the adjustments became bolder and more elaborate, in the manner of a stage director's wilder interpretation of a time-worn play. The siege of Troy in the garden at Bulaq Dakhrur, with the gardeners as the opposing forces – except of course that they didn't know about the casting. And later still I acquired the hubris to supply my own sequels and parallel developments. Penelope did not in fact sit meekly awaiting Ulysses – she took up with one of the suitors, who was far better-looking anyway, and sailed away with him to found a rival establishment from whence Ulysses would in turn attempt to haul her back. And so on. Until at last I learned to break away from the models and spin private fantasies with some claim to originality.

But never, of course, an absolute claim. Children do indeed start out as literary innocents but the innocence is fragile. Corruption – so to speak – sets in with exposure to structured language of any kind. Prose, poetry. Fairy stories, mythology. Fiction, comics, Arabella Buckley. When I set my own seven-year-old effort beside the hundreds of pieces of unfettered writing by primary-school children in this country that I read in the course of judging that children's writing competition, I see it as a dire instance of what happens when a child arrives early at a concept of what writing ought to be. But influence is inescapable. Numbers of those primary-school children were writing poetry that had a strong flavour of Ted Hughes. No bad thing, I hasten to say — but a demonstration of the way in which the pristine approach to language is contaminated as soon as the child hears or sees a story, a poem, contrived language of any kind at all. It cannot be otherwise, and one would not wish it otherwise. Children must learn to read, and to write. The exciting thing about the writing of younger children is the way in which so many manage to incorporate influences while retaining a freshness and idiosyncrasy. That individual vision survives, for a while.

So that was early education, for me. It seems now to have been in one way ideal and in another way crippling. There is no knowing if I would have turned out a bookish child anyway or was shunted in that direction by solitude and the requirements of the PNEU. Whatever — I ended up at twelve as a fervent reader, with a capacity for application and an assumption that learning was on the whole enjoyable. When eventually I went to my first school, in England, I was well up to standard in all areas except Maths and Latin, both of which needed some urgent repair work. But I was woefully short on social skills. The disadvantages of all that indulgent one-to-one attention are obvious. I had never learned alongside another child, indeed had had very little to do with other children. I was introspective and good at being alone – not qualities that come in handy at an English girls' boarding school. Flung into that fetid jungle I was lost. I knew none of the strategies of survival. Alternatively exhilarated and alarmed by the sudden exposure to this horde, I flailed around like an untrained puppy, and invited dislike. Children sense an outsider, and I was that all right. Eventually, I learned a stoical endurance but, where learning was concerned, the sun had now gone in.

Hitherto, I had been growing up in the belief that books were enjoyable. I was quite prepared to have a go at anything. But now I found myself amid other adolescents most of whom held reading in contempt, an attitude that was subtly connived at by the teachers. The charismatic figures in the school were the good games players. Those who prospered academically were accorded a form of cool token approval along with which went the unspoken comment that they were on the whole dull fish. One of the punishments was to be sent to read for an hour in the library. You had to select a book, read, and then report on what you had read to the duty teacher. A sinister distortion of the PNEU system. The library contained little anyway except a few battered encyclopedias.

I was by then too deeply steeped in heresy to recant. I accepted, grimly, that I was cherishing a perversion and went underground. I read under the bedclothes at night, and on the rare occasions when I could find a secluded corner and thought that no one was looking. I got found out, of course. Pious dormitory prefects reported me. My copy of *The Oxford Book of English Verse* was confiscated from my locker by an assiduous matron and returned to me in a reproving private interview with the headmistress. She pushed the book across her desk towards me — assertive red-tipped talons lay on the dark blue binding — 'There is no need for you to read this sort of thing in your spare time, Penelope. You will be *taught* all that.' She went on to point out that my lacrosse skills were abysmally below par.

I grew up, after what seemed like several centuries, and found my way at last into the sunlight of a university where I discovered to my surprise that lots of other eighteen-year-olds had been reading quite openly for years.

Chapter Six

We are driving from Cairo to Alexandria along the Desert Road. The car has been fitted out with its thick squashy desert tyres for the occasion. The road reaches away ahead and behind like a black ribbon, narrowing where sand has drifted almost across it. We pass an army convoy, a long slow-moving chain of lorries and tank-carriers and the occasional jeep or armoured car. We edge past them one by one and I count them as we go, with the window open and the hot sandy wind rushing through the car. I wave to the soldiers and some of them wave back. They sit crammed in the backs of lorries — smoking, waving.

We have been driving for hours, days. I keep asking when we will get to the Half Way House, where there are cold drinks and lavatories. I am in need of both.

The journey along the desert route to Alexandria probably did take many hours. It is about 140 miles, and nowadays the road is dual carriageway, but back then it was a narrow track of tarmac which dissolved here and there into a sandy waste, depending on how recent the last high winds had been. Hence the desert tyres. We could have gone by train. The railway between Cairo and Alexandria was built by Robert Stephenson and opened in 1856, vastly contributing to the influx of European visitors to Cairo and Upper Egypt. It was a side-shoot of the European and American railway boom and must have been one of the earliest railways on the African continent. I certainly remember it – the bedlam of the station, and then the trains which always started late and reproduced all gradations of social and cultural life – the first class with separate compartments and upholstered seats and a dining-car, and then the second and third with slatted wooden benches and people carry-ing bunches of live chickens, and finally the roof and the couplings to which clung the free-loaders, a tattered swarm of men and boys clutching on to each other if they couldn't achieve a handhold on the train. We must then have used the railway on occasion, but it is the drive along the Desert Road that retains its mystique. The sand, the wind, the Half Way House, the beginning of the Alexandrian summer.

We went in May, when the temperature in Cairo began to soar, and came back in September. It was a serious annual migration. It took place before the war, in the years when we did not go to England, because I have photographs which show me sitting in the Mediter-ranean as a plump infant, and leaping boldly from a houseboat into Alexandria harbour, wearing water wings made out of gourds. I don't remember those times, but the early years of the war are quite clear. We were certainly there in 1940 and 1941. The annual exodus to Alexandria was far too important a feature of expatriate Cairo life to be affected by a passing inconvenience like the Libyan campaign. We moved to Alexandria nicely in time for the bombing of the city. Cairo, of course, was never bombed.

In fact the bombing of Alexandria was concentrated on the harbour region, some distance from the residential area in which my mother would rent a villa for the summer. Indeed, for me the air raids simply added to the festive atmosphere of the place and gave it a further esoteric dimension. The sky was suffused with fireworks. If the raid was bad you were got out of bed and tucked up in a rug under the dining-room table, and there was always the possibility of picking up shrapnel in the garden next morning.

I loved Alex. To go there was to be translated into another world – a faster, brighter, shinier world of sun and wind and sea. There was the Corniche, that ran the length of the seafront, with rusty railings that stained the hands orange and below the tumbled concrete cubes of breakwaters and beyond that the sea, rushing up in columns of foam. There were the leisurely streets of villas set in leafy gardens. And the city centre, a tram-ride away, with expensive shops and Baudrot's, which was the Alexandria equivalent to Groppi's, with cakes and ices that were if possible even superior. And, above all, there were the beaches.

Stanley Bay. The Military Beach. Sidi Bishr No. 1 and
Sidi Bishr No. 2 and Sidi Bishr No. 3. Significantly
different one from another. Stanley Bay was distinctly
down-market – a huge semi-circle of beach huts giving
on to concrete promenades – crowded, cosmopolitan
and lively, with itinerant peanut sellers and gully-gully
men, who did conjuring tricks with live baby chickens.
Lucy and I were sometimes reduced to Stanley Bay
because it was within walking distance of our home
base. The Military Beach was also within easy reach and
held in somewhat low esteem because there was not
much sand, just shingle and pebbles. I was partial to the
Military Beach: the fishing was excellent. There was a
rich system of shallow reefs and rock pools stretching
away to sea for a hundred yards or more, and a long
breakwater fingering right out into deep water. The
breakwater was on the whole for serious, adult anglers,
but one could lurk behind them, gawping at their ma-
jestic catch. I fished in the rock pools, scooping my net
under the overhangs to bring it up jumping with
shrimps. Tiny ones, for the most part, but there was
always the possibility of a whopper – translucent, with
those black blobs of eyes, throbbing in the palm of my
hand. Sometimes it was rod-and-line stuff, squatting for
hours on a rock watching my float, until the heady
moment when it began to dip and circle. There was a
kind of silvery triangular fish with black bands on the
tail, that lived in shoals, and among the rocks and
seaweed there were rockfish, with sucker-like mouths. I

did not care for these, and there was always a problem about getting them off the hook. Lucy washed her hands of this, so I would tramp the beach in search of assistance. It was a place much frequented by courting couples – soldiers and sailors with their girls – Greek girls, French girls, Lebanese girls, ATS and WAAFS and WRNS. I would select a likely pair and stand over them, an insistent figure in sagging navy-blue woollen bathing costume and white cotton sun-hat, proffering a slimy creature on the end of a nylon line. I must have blighted many an afternoon of dalliance.

Actually, my approach to marine life was ambivalent. When it was on a small scale I was fascinated. The delicate pink and green sea-anemones whose tentacles had a tacky feel if you stuck your finger in them: I fed them shrimps, sadistically. And the tiny skittering sand-crabs, light as feathers, that blew in shoals across the sand in front of the advancing waves. The cowrie shells you could find along the tide-line and the little leathery dead starfish. The clouds of tiny fish that would skim across a pool, flashing silver in the sun. It was the lurking menace of monstrosity that I feared – overtones of that Nile catfish. Once, fishing on my own far out on the reef, I disturbed something two or three feet long which whipped away from pool to pool in a great dark powerful rush. Swimming in deep water, there was always the thought that some sinister mass might come wheeling up from far below.

*

Above: PL in 1938 – posing dourly for a Cairo street photographer

Below: Bulaq Dakhrur during PL's childhood

Above: A wartime wedding party at Bulaq Dakhrur

Above right: A convoy on the desert road

Below right: A neat – if somewhat contrived – juxtaposition. The donkey lines and the Pyramid climbers seem to have been cleared away for the occasion

Above: General de Gaulle in Cairo in April 1941. General Wavell on the left, General Catroux (Free French Commander in the Middle East) on the right

Above right: Street scene in Alexandria. A WREN and her companion enjoying their leave

Below right: PL in a tree at Mount Carmel, Palestine, in 1942

Above: Gezira Sporting Club. The occasion is a particular one – a tea-party for repatriated prisoners of war in 1943 – but the scene is typical: the socializing crowd, the attendant *suffragis*

Above right: Archeological remains of the Bulaq Dakhrur swimming pool in 1984

Below right: PL outside Bulaq Dakhrur in February 1984

St Paul's amid the rubble in 1941. By the time I saw it in 1945 the
Royal Engineers had long since finished clearing up the débris, and
the willowherb had grown, but the effect was much the same

The water is just below waist level, which is precisely right. Any higher, and I would not be able to push off with my feet at the crucial moment. I have to be able to lean forward and launch myself with a kick at the exact moment that the wave is breaking.

I stand facing the shore with my head turned, assessing each approaching wave, clutching the surfboard. If they have already broken they are no good to me. Those that are still swelling must be allowed to go, lifting me temporarily off my feet as they do so. What I am after is the one that is ripening to a peak which frills with white as it begins to turn in on itself. Then I can fling myself forward with it and if the timing is right I will swoop down the slope of water and hurtle in with the wave – a glorious involuntary rush which will leave me washed up on the beach.

Out of the corner of my eye I can see Lucy. She is waving. Not in greeting but in summons. I am to come out. I pretend I have not seen her. I go on waiting my moment. Great white broken waves charge through me. I bob up and down with the swells. And then the right one comes, and I have timed it right, the wave has me in its grip, and I am racing for the beach.

The wave dies, and deposits me on the sand. Lucy is looking thunder, and I brace myself for an earful.

This was not, I hasten to say, surfing on a Hawaiian scale. There were adults who were doing ostentatious things with proper surfboards, way out in the deep water. My surfboard was a child's version of the kind most surfing camp-followers used – an oblong board with a rounded end over which you placed your hands, shaped to the waist at the other. Mine was made to measure, and had my initials on it in green paint – P.M.L. It was my most treasured possession. I was a good swimmer, and fancied myself as a surfer. I was passionate about it. I saw waves in my dreams, flaunting those alluring glassy flanks. When we went to the surfing beach I was in a state of tension, awaiting the colour of the flag. No flag meant no danger, and therefore possibly no waves either. Red meant hazardous, and therefore good waves, but an argument with Lucy about the degree of hazard. Black meant swimming forbidden.

Lucy never bathed. She would set up an encampment on the sand – sun umbrella, rug and stool, Thermos flask, knitting – and from there she would supervise my activities. If we had access to a beach cabin, as tenants or guests, she would base herself in the greater comfort of the cabin, with its benches and shade, and make forays to check up on me. The surfing beach was Sidi Bishr No. 3, where we never had a cabin, so Lucy must have been condemned to many an afternoon's edgy patrolling of the shore while I plunged off into the Mediterranean. Occasionally, when my flouting of her shouts and waves became entirely blatant, she would despatch some total stranger to admonish me. And once, the *gaffir* – the beach watchman – who came racing out with a life-belt and hauled me back: an appalling humiliation.

I have every sympathy with Lucy, now. I'd do the same myself. A few people drowned off that beach every summer. According to Lucy it was because they'd gone into the water too soon after eating their lunch or their tea, which gave you cramp. I had to sit fretting on the sand for an hour after ingestion. I remember once seeing a tarpaulin stretched out on the sand with an oblong shape beneath, and a muttering crowd standing about. There were lifebelts tethered to posts every hundred yards or so, and those *gaffirs* in navy shorts and sweaters, who howled imprecations at anyone breaking the black-flag rule. In fact, I knew about the treachery of the inviting water, but I never let on to anyone. Once I had been caught in a current in the trough of deep water fifty yards from the shore, and found myself pulled terrifyingly out to sea. And on several occasions I had misjudged the size of a wave or positioned myself wrongly and turned head over heels, banging against the surfboard, caught up helplessly, hideously, in a roaring cauldron of water. I kept an expedient silence about such things. Surfing was essential; surfing was the whole point of existence. I have never surfed since, but I have always felt a sneaking empathy with those obsessives who traipse the globe in search of waves. I knew how they feel, once.

The beaches, like the trains, reflected the complexities of class and culture. Stanley Bay was raffish and multi-cultural. The Military Beach was domestic, despite the courting couples. Sidi Bishr No. 1 was plebeian. Sidi

Bishr No. 3 was dashing and classy. Sidi Bishr No. 2 was classier yet, and it was there that my mother tried to achieve a beach cabin, each summer. Whether this was done by lottery, by order of application or by corruption I have no idea. The last, I should guess. Whatever – it was a matter of anxious anticipation. One year, Lucy and I concocted an April Fool trick whereby we announced that while she was out a man had phoned to say that she had a cabin allocated in the prime position in the centre of the beach, front row. My mother was ecstatic. 'April Fool!' I shouted, triumphant. Her reaction was explosive. Beach cabins were serious matters – definitions of status, and the focus of the summer's social life.

They were little detached villas on wooden stilts, painted cream and green, with a covered veranda in the front and a flight of wooden steps leading down to the sand. I seem to remember about three ranks of them, at both Sidi Bishr Nos. 2 and 3; front row was the most desirable – from there you could observe the comings and goings of the beach and accost your friends. Drinks, lunch and tea parties were held on the veranda. Towels and bathing costumes were hung out to dry on the surrounding railings. Inside, you changed, and kept all the summer equipment – the surfboards and the sun umbrellas and the buckets and spades.

It was the area underneath the cabins that interested me – cool wastelands in which accumulated an enticing detritus of garbage. I was not allowed to go there, for fear of broken glass, but did so, repeatedly. I can summon up that landscape now, with no difficulty at all. There was a clearance of a couple of feet or so only, so you had to crawl, or shuffle forward on your stomach. Sand that was chill instead of burning like the beach sand. Strips of light between the planks of the cabin floor above. If you lay on your back under the veranda part you could see the pink slices of people's feet and listen to conversations. And there was a treasure-trove of rubbish. Bottle tops, which I collected, and chunks of milky-green glass washed smooth by the sea. Crisp ribbons of brown seaweed. Cigarette ends. White cuttlefish. Gobs of blackish tar. Little wooden ice-cream spoons. Matchboxes. Sea-urchin shells. Buttons. And occasionally some mystifying object which might require identification. Once I interrupted one of my mother's cabin At Homes brandishing a curiously structured burst balloon. There was an outbreak of feverishly inconsequential chatter and I was sent packing, condom and all.

The attraction of Sidi Bishr No. 2 was that the beach was sheltered by a long low rocky island two or three hundred yards offshore. The channel between thus offered calm, safe swimming. Furthermore, you could swim out to the island and explore. It had a shallow lagoon in the middle, full of wonders – tiny jewel-like green crabs and the biggest shrimps in creation and a kind of red starfish that I never saw anywhere else. I thought of it as a miraculous otherworld, and had a long-running fantasy narrative in which I lived there,

alone, a sort of female Robinson Crusoe with the romantic overtones of Nausicaa or Andromeda. The seaward
side of the island sloped up to a low cliff, an awkward
climb in bare feet over sharp rocks and pools of slippery
weed but essential, because from the cliff you looked out
to the open sea – crashing against the island and reaching
away in a great blue quilt to the horizon, on which
perched the grey cut-out of a cruiser or an aircraft
carrier. The island was a nirvana. When I was very small
I was towed out to it clinging to my father's back. Later
I could struggle there myself, doing a splashy breast-
stroke and wearing gourds. And eventually I could
swim all the way, easily, gourdless and mature.

In good years we had a cabin at Sidi Bishr No. 2,
whence you could walk along the beach and thence on
to the concrete promenade to Sidi Bishr No. 3, with its
own townscape of beach cabins, ranging from an outer
suburbia at the extreme edges to the prime positions in
the centre front. In bad years we had no cabin and had
to establish an enclave of sun umbrellas, or cadge invita-
tions. Lucy and I were occasionally bidden to join the
children of a wealthy Anglo-French family, acquaintances
of my parents, who had a permanent cabin on Sidi Bishr
No. 3 – the equivalent of membership of the Athenaeum.
The children and their attendants were brought to the
beach in a chauffeur-driven car, from which the chauffeur
then carried to the cabin the beribboned boxes of cakes
from Baudrot's which were the substance of the picnic
tea. Their cabin had a table, on which the tea was set

out, and a set of folding chairs. There were paper plates, and patterned paper serviettes, and iced lemonade. There would be one of those big chocolate cakes topped with sugar-dusted chocolate logs, macaroons, cream-filled pastry boats, éclairs. And I would sit there slavering, a shameless hanger-on, a serf at the baronial feast, anxious only to get my paws on anything going. When *we* had a beach picnic it was Marmite sandwiches and a banana.

There was beach life, and there was villa life — the long, leisurely mornings playing in our garden or in someone else's. The gardens were richer and lusher than the gardens of Cairo, of Zamalek, even Bulaq Dakhrur itself. And there were chameleons in them. They stalked the branches of trees and shrubs, mysterious aliens with swivelling eyes and three-fingered hands like cool gloves. They seemed like manifestations of some fantasy world, leading their slow-motion lives in there among the leaves, hanging in frozen postures, or inching forward, out of kilter with everything else — the birds and the flickering lizards and the black trickle of ants on a tree trunk. A whole mythology attached to them: they could change colour according to background, if you put them on something multicoloured they would explode. I would scour the bushes for them, the little brown ones and the large bright green ones. I liked to hold them and then stare intently at them — the slack bellies that fluttered as they breathed, the perfect spiral of the coiled tail. They clung to my finger and hissed with open mouths. Lucy was repelled by them and admonished: they would bite, they were probably poisonous. I ignored her, and tried to test the mythologies. I put the brown ones on the lawn, but they stayed resolutely brown. I put a green one in the pocket of my pink dress, but when I took it out it was as green as ever. I considered a definitive experiment involving Lucy's knitting bag, a rainbow affair of yellow shading through to red, but could never bring myself to carry it out. Suppose the creature really did explode?

It was in Alex that I first had to wear glasses, realized that I had freckles, and was mistaken for a boy. The three things are fused into one dismaying event. My father – affectionately, teasingly, meaning no harm at all – called me 'freckle-face'. I rushed to a mirror, and saw that he was quite right. For the rest of the summer (or the week, or the day) I was ablaze with self-consciousness. If anyone's gaze fell on me they were looking, I knew, at my freckles. I was blighted. And then (next day, next week, next month) I was taken to an oculist who diagnosed short sight and astigmatism. I was furnished with spectacles, for lessons and for reading. I knew no other child who had to wear spectacles. Now I was disabled as well as blighted. And Lucy had knitted me a bathing costume which was only a pair of trunks without the customary additional rectangle that vaguely covered the chest and tied round the neck with a tape. I was bared from the waist up, like a boy. Furthermore, my hair had been cut very short. The inevitable happened. Someone at a beach gathering took me for a boy:

'Would he like another sandwich?' The surge of embarrassment and affront was greater than any I had ever known – or indeed, it now seems, than any since. Bespectacled, freckled and hermaphrodite, I soldiered through that summer.

The freckles and the spectacles are still with me; I have long since come to terms with both. But those Alexandrian summers still bubble to the surface in another way – small skin eruptions called solar keratosis which periodically appear and have to be spirited away by a dermatologist. Sunshine decades old is locked into my body, with unstoppable effects.

Our last summer in Alexandria was 1944. By then my father had been transferred to the Sudan branch of his bank and my mother was mostly absent also, preoccupied with the man who would become her second husband. There was no rented villa. Lucy and I lodged with an elderly bachelor banking acquaintance of my father's, whom we never saw. His Lebanese housekeeper Josephine, a huge, cushion-like lady with gold teeth, spoiled me rotten and cooked us wonderful meals. I discovered that the rest of the world did not eat rice pudding and macaroni cheese and stewed prunes. I was eleven now, as tall as Lucy, and sobering up. I no longer flirted with naval officers. Lucy and I went for long walks along the Corniche, and read *Tom Sawyer* to each other in the evenings. There was something unspoken – a sense that we were on the edge of things. I thought that probably I would never be in Alexandria again, and I was right, almost.

When at last I went back, in 1988, I was incredulous. It was not that the place had changed. Quite simply, it had gone. Vanished. Obliterated. It was as though the whole thing had been a mirage – the airy, elegant villas brilliant with bougainvillaea that rose from the gardens of palms and tamarisk and oleander, the golden curves of the beaches, the long, leisurely parade of the Corniche following the great curve of the shoreline. In its place there was a wasteland of concrete stumps, stretching in all directions. The entire place had been built yesterday, it seemed – a lunar landscape of stark apartment blocks, mile upon mile. It made me think of the outskirts of Moscow. I was driven from end to end of the city, staring out of the car window in a state of shock. This was a transformation far beyond that of Cairo, where the old bones of the place still showed through. Here there was nothing, *nothing*. It seemed beyond belief that an entire landscape could be expunged in forty years. The highway that roared the length of the coastline must be following the line of the Corniche. But where were the beaches? An empty, unidentifiable expanse. The sea was so polluted, I was told, that no one in their right mind would venture into it. At one point a circular bite seemed perhaps to reflect the site of Stanley Bay. I searched in vain for the island off Sidi Bishr No. 2. Could they have wiped out that too? Ranks of concrete block-houses dumped on the sand were perhaps a mockery of the beach huts. There was not a tree to be seen. The place was drowned in concrete. The sky was sulphur-coloured, and there was a curious metallic smell. I spent a disconsolate night in the Montazah Sheraton, with incipient bronchitis, and iron in the soul, feeling as though my own past had been sliced away.

The Alexandria of the 1930s and 1940s survives now only in my mind, and in the minds of others. Most of whom knew it a great deal better than I did. For I did not know it at all, I realize, any more than I knew Cairo in any real sense. Much of it I never even saw – the densely populated slum quarters to the west of the city, the labyrinthine streets of downtown Alexandria, tucked behind the boulevards and shops. It was not one city but half a dozen, in which people moved on different planes, segregated by class and culture. And for me there was the further segregation of childhood. My Alexandria was a sybaritic dream. Peanuts in a paper cone, eaten on the Corniche. The suck and whoosh of the sea at the Spouting Rock. The milky-green curve of a surfing wave. The cool grip of a chameleon. Pistachio ice-cream. Macaroons. A medley of allusions, which add up now to a place which no longer exists in any sense at all.

It is not quite true to say that everything has gone. Shreds survive, here and there. Before the bronchitic night at the Montazah Sheraton I had walked out along the promontory to the Mameluke fort which is on the site of the Pharos, visited the Graeco-Roman Museum and spent the evening at a party in a lavishly ornate villa whose interior achieved that same curious combination of Moorish–Edwardian as Mena House. But this was to step into other Alexandrias which I sensed as a child but could in no way identify. Alexandria was then, and had always been, a Mediterranean city. It looked out, to the sea, not inwards, to Africa. It was not so much Islamic as a glorious hybrid, owing most of all to its Greek heritage. Its population was strongly Greek. And Jewish and Lebanese and Coptic and Maltese and French. The streets were called Rue Rouchdi, Rue Rowlatt, instead of Sharia this and that. To travel that brief distance up the Delta was to have moved into another culture as well as another climate. Several cultures, and above all one that was *sui generis*, unlike anywhere else before or since and extinguished now along with that ephemeral and transient landscape. I brushed against it, busy with my surfboard and my chameleons, and got a whiff of something pungent and unique.

Every city is in one sense a construct of the imagination. It is seen differently by each pair of eyes, reinterpreted through the lens of knowledge, of beliefs, of affiliations. And Alexandria, above all others, seems a city fated to be seen as a concept rather than a reality. The site of the vanished library of antiquity, the haunt of Cleopatra, a literary vision. Contemporary Alexandrians would quarrel – understandably enough – with the notion that their city does not exist, but it is an uneasy truth. Reading Lawrence Durrell today I cannot find anything much to evoke the Alexandria I knew – just the occasional emotive name – Ras el Tin, Mareotis,

Aboukir, Glymenopoulos — and here and there a clutch of words through which gleams a reflection of the place: trams shuddering in their thin metal veins, white drifts of sand along the slats of Venetian shutters.

But this is hardly surprising. I did not move in such circles. And indeed *The Alexandria Quartet* seems to me a fiction that is not so much an evocation of a city as the statement of a concept of sexual behaviour. The place is an emanation of the characters, and as such a fiction in a further sense. But it remains for most of its readers the inescapable definition of the city of Alexandria. No city has been more subsumed into literature — a city of the mind in every sense. In the end, it seems grimly appropriate that the mirage city should have been entirely superseded by a concrete wilderness.

Chapter Seven

When I was nine I saw Charles de Gaulle in his dressing-gown. I see him still, quite clear and precise, dressing-gown and all. I know where, too, and why.

Lucy and I are staying at Government House in Jerusalem. My mother is not. She is staying at the American Colony *pension*. Lucy and I are thus privileged because before Lucy came to look after me, long ago, she looked after the daughters of the High Commissioner and his wife. We have a room which opens off a long corridor, and further along the corridor is the bathroom which we use. We have to share this bathroom with General de Gaulle, who is also staying at Government House. We must not loiter in the bathroom, lest we impede the General, and we must keep out of his way. Also, his presence here is a secret. It is hush-hush. We must not mention the matter to anyone. But we peer round our door and hence I see General de Gaulle lope along the corridor on his way to the bathroom, an immensely tall figure, stately, with very long white legs beneath the dressing-gown, which is patterned in a design of swirls and curves. He carries a sponge.

Paisley, the dressing-gown, it now seems to me. I didn't know that at the time – I wouldn't have known what paisley was – but memory obligingly records that swirling pattern which the wisdoms of today interpret as paisley. The colour is more elusive. There is an impression of darkness and richness, but there it stops. That is as far as I can go on Charles de Gaulle's dressing-gown.

And now I am confronted with an interesting collision between the firm statement in my head and the equally firm statements of recorded history. The Free French leader was indeed in the Middle East in 1942. Both his own memoirs and the accounts of his various biographers affirm that he arrived in Cairo on 21 July, whence he proceeded in August to Damascus and Beirut, where he was based until his return to London at the end of September. There is no mention of any visit to Jerusalem. However, the year before, in June 1941, he was most certainly in Jerusalem, according to the memoirs.

So far as my own movements are concerned, common sense would suggest that we were in Palestine in the late summer and autumn of 1942, in the wake of 'The Flap' and the run-up to the battle of Alamein which took place at the beginning of November. We did indeed visit Palestine at other times, both before and after, but it does not seem likely that we would have gone there in the early summer of 1941, when the situation in Syria was precarious. Syria was under French mandate and was the Middle Eastern base of the pro-Vichy French army. The Germans had made landings there in the spring of 1941, and General Wavell, in Cairo, was under pressure from both London and from the Free French leader to open a Syrian campaign. In June a combined British, Australian and Free French force moved into Syria, which is why General de Gaulle then arrived in Jerusalem. He had personally taken command of the Middle Eastern Free French forces and was anxious to follow up a successful attack on the German force with a patriotic summons to his own fellow-countrymen. In the event, the Germans pulled out before any engagement took place, and de Gaulle and his associates faced a hostile and humiliating reception from the Vichy forces. In July Syria came under Allied control. Given all this, I cannot think that my mother would have decided on Palestine as an inviting venue for a summer holiday in early 1941.

But we were certainly there in 1942. General de Gaulle was in the area, in August – that is clear enough. He was in Damascus and Beirut – no great distance from Jerusalem. And there is that telling little detail in my mental picture: secrecy, the injunctions about discretion.

Three possibilities. I never saw the General at all, but have concocted this strange image in response to some bizarre prompting of the psyche. It happened, but in 1941. It happened in 1942, in which case I offer the episode to de Gaulle scholars as a provocative footnote:

that in August 1942 the Free French leader made a brief and probably clandestine visit to Jerusalem, lodged at Government House, and that his presence was recorded by a pair of beady nine-year-old eyes. Along with his choice of dressing-gown.

I favour the third possibility, and indeed it is tempting now to furnish the General with some thoughts as he headed for the bathroom, sponge in hand. He would have been in a state of elation in the wake of the events of early June, when the Free French force based in Egypt had been in action for the first time with the Eighth Army and had held a key position on the southern flank of the retreating British in the face of Rommel's onslaught. The French had hung on for fourteen days at Bir Hacheim, a stand which was seen at the time as a strategic success and which was hailed as a valiant feat of arms on the part of the Free French. De Gaulle would still have been glowing about that, but his head would also have been filled with baleful thoughts about perfidious Albion. He was at loggerheads with Churchill, and the Middle East had already been the scene of at least one of his more spirited exchanges with British representatives. He had had a notorious row in 1941 in Cairo with Oliver Lyttelton, Minister of State for the Middle East, over the position of the Free French in Syria, convinced that the British were intent upon manoeuvring the French out of the Levant and with his eye already upon the post-war role of France. He would have been worrying about the strength of Rommel's position, poised on the borders of Libya and Egypt, but also jealously protective of French interests. Whatever business he was about in Jerusalem, he cannot have been an easy guest at Government House.

Palestine. Government House. It sounds like another age, as indeed it was. In Jerusalem, these were the last years of the British mandate, an uneasy time. The whole Arab–Jewish question was on the boil, and Britain was mistrusted by both sides. The Palestinians bitterly resented the Balfour Declaration with its approval of the establishment of a Jewish national home in Palestine and saw the British mandate as legitimizing and fostering Zionist settlement. The Zionists considered Britain to be equivocal in its policy and were enraged by the restrictions placed on Jewish land purchases in 1939. By 1942 the more extreme Zionists were openly opposed to Britain, and guerrilla warfare was being carried out against the British by the terrorist Irgun and Stern groups. Government House bristled with security arrangements, quite unconnected with the visit of General de Gaulle.

All our visits to Palestine are now conflated, in the mind's eye. There is a sequence of slides – places, events – but none of them can be tethered to a year or a month except General de Gaulle and his dressing-gown, by the fortuitous intervention of history. And there must be a whisper of doubt, even there. Like Alexandria, Jerusalem is now a busy, kaleidoscopic impression, along with everywhere else in the Palestine to which we went – somehow and at some point.

In 1942 we travelled there by train, I think. We must have been a part of that exodus from Cairo in June and July and August, when the German advance had begun to look distinctly threatening. I have always thought that we did not leave until almost the eve of Alamein, perhaps in mid-October, but if we coincided with the General in Jerusalem in August, then it must have been earlier. Again, history lends a hand. So it would have been in the swelter of midsummer that we packed into the crowded train that ran to Ismailiya, where you crossed the Suez canal by ferry and took a further train to Jerusalem. And I remember nothing of it at all.

It is the drives across Sinai that I remember. Several, probably, fused into one. The long straight road. The rolling sand dunes that go on for ever, with every now and then, miles from anywhere, the solitary figure of an Arab. Walking. Doing what? Going where? Clumps of some dry spiny shrub. Spinning balls of tumbleweed. Rusty petrol cans by the roadside. Stopping to have a pee – the mandatory retreat from the road lest another car should pass and see you, the trek off into the desert in search of a concealing contour.

There was always the interesting possibility of a puncture. A great lark, to my mind, because that meant an unscheduled stop of indeterminate length, awaiting rescue. A patch of shade was contrived by making a lean-to against the car with the piled luggage from the boot and the picnic rug, and there we would huddle until after half an hour or so (half a day, two days . . .) a puff of dust on the horizon indicated an approaching vehicle. Usually an army jeep or lorry which would furnish an amiable soldier who set to and changed the tyre while Lucy supplied sandwiches and tea and my mother proffered cigarettes. Once we brought an entire convoy to a halt in this way. Everyone disembarked and brewed up at the side of the road and I struck up an intense relationship with a sergeant who let me sit at the wheel of a tank-carrier.

The canal was like a sea, so wide you could hardly see across, or so it now seems. There was a tumultuous ferry, and the babel of the dock at Ismailiya, with clamouring porters and men selling carpets and slippers and fly-whisks and boys who dived into the canal after piastres thrown by people on the waiting ships. I remember above all the customs-shed, always the scene of vivid altercations between my mother and Egyptian customs officials. On one occasion the matter at issue was tortoises. I had – in a shoe box with holes carefully drilled in the lid – two treasured Palestinian tortoises gathered on the slopes of the Mount of Olives. With these, I intended to embark on some selective breeding. My own tortoises at Bulaq Dakhrur were the Algerian variety – agreeable but supine creatures. The Palestinian variety were small, dark-shelled, manic animals that could move at the rate of knots, raising themselves on all four scaly points and surging across the hillsides like little tanks. It had struck me that if I mixed these tortoises up with my own the results might be interesting. Besides, my own were not good breeders – they laid eggs, but the eggs never hatched, however assiduously I supplied them with sandy undisturbed nurseries. Clearly, what was needed was an introduction of fresh new stock. With this in mind, I had clambered with Lucy over the hillsides around Jerusalem until at last we found and captured this precious pair.

My mother duly declared the tortoises on the customs form. The customs official pounced: 'It is forbidden to import insects into Egypt.' My mother retaliated in triumph that these were not insects, these were reptiles. The customs official dived into an office and returned with a grubby handbook. Now it was his turn to crow: reptiles also are forbidden. There was an excited argument. I burst into tears.

And then suddenly the problem was resolved. The official shrugged and waved us through. My tears? Or did my mother slip him fifty piastres? Whatever happened, the tortoises made it into Egypt and eventually to Bulaq Dakhrur, where they beat up the resident tortoises and eventually escaped into the cultivation. Presumably tortoise species do not interbreed.

That summer of 1942 we were forever on the move, in Palestine. Tel Aviv. Jaffa. Haifa. Nahariya. Mount Carmel. The names are strung out still in my head, with hazy images attached. Tel Aviv is an overcrowded beach and some fuss about hotel rooms – Lucy perturbed and my mother locked in conflict with someone at a reception desk. Jaffa is a car breakdown: a long wait at a garage where a mechanic lies under the car with his legs protruding, and I sit under a tree eating pistachio nuts out of a paper bag, which is not normally permitted. Mount Carmel is a tree, a tree which I climbed, daily for what seems weeks on end, a great city of a tree with a labyrinth of trunks and branches, fat dependable limbs up which I could swarm, up and up.

Thus is it reduced, that complex and explosive country. Subsumed into the fragments of my own concerns. There is a landscape, also, but a landscape which is remarkable mainly because it is not the landscape of Egypt. Hills. Grey-green hills with olive trees and rocky outcrops. Miles of orange groves, apparently growing in sand. Wild flowers on those hillsides – little irises, and thyme and bushes of rosemary. To this day, the smell of the rosemary in my Oxfordshire garden says Palestine.

Did I understand anything of what was going on there? I suspect not. There were resonances, for sure, but they were not the resonances of the Arab–Jewish conflict or of the controversial nature of the British mandate. They were once again the resonances of personal reference. I was a child reared on the Bible, and here we were on the identifiable territory of the biblical narrative. This seemed to be some sort of confirmation of the veracity of the whole thing, but at the same time it was vaguely unsatisfactory. It was not what I had expected. I had furnished the Bible stories with a mental backcloth of my own, just as I had constructed scenarios for Greek mythology, and now here we were in the middle of the real thing and it was cluttered with extraneous detail. Jerusalem was full of cars and lorries. Nazareth had a café that sold Kia Ora fruit juice. The Sea of Galilee had a beach with sun umbrellas and children with buckets and spades. Bethlehem . . . Ah, Bethlehem.

I am in the very grand car of the High Commissioner. We are going to Bethlehem. The High Commissioner and his wife have to go there on some official duty and Lucy and I have been allowed to come too, for the experience. Lucy has told me that this is a very special privilege, and I must behave impeccably. I behave impeccably. I sit in silence beside Lucy in the back of the big car. There is a chauffeur in uniform driving and someone else in uniform alongside. There are outriders on motor bikes fore and aft and an armoured car bringing up the rear. We are a cavalcade, which sweeps slowly along a road that winds through the hills.

It comes to me that I need to go to the lavatory. I convey my need to Lucy. Lucy whispers to the High Commissioner's wife, requesting that the car be called to a halt, briefly, so that Penelope may go behind a bush. The High Commissioner's wife replies crisply that this is not possible.

Grimly, I clench my knees together and hope for the best. I sit bolt upright, staring ahead in order to concentrate the mind, feeling martyred and heroic. Lucy shoots reproachful glances at the High Commissioner's wife. Bethlehem, I do not notice.

*

The High Commissioner, Sir Harold MacMichael, would have been at the time a prime target of the extreme Zionist terrorist groups. Two years later the Minister of State in Cairo, Lord Moyne, was assassinated by members of the Stern group. The craggy landscape through which we drove had rocky outcrops at either side of the road – excellent terrorist country. Lady MacMichael's reaction seems entirely reasonable. And knowing what I now know I can account for other phenomena which neither interested nor concerned me at the time – the rash of Military Police in the streets of Jerusalem, the sentries with rifles who popped up all over the hillsides around Government House and, on occasion, advised about promising locations for tortoise hunts.

Jerusalem is also reduced to a smell – incense. The Church of the Holy Sepulchre: milling crowds and men chanting, invisible, and that richly exotic smell, doctrinal and mysterious. Once more, this had nothing to do with the familiar and controllable landscape of the King James Bible and the Authorized Version of the Prayer Book. Lucy, a paid-up Christian, was stirred and uplifted by the Holy Sepulchre, though probably dismayed by the incense, as a good Protestant. I trailed around beside her, obscurely offended. Cairo Cathedral was one thing, this suggested impenetrable mysteries, and I was alienated.

My mother stayed in a hotel-*pension* called the American Colony. It was a modest establishment with a long low building around a courtyard with orange trees, lavender and rosemary bushes, and was much favoured on account of its cheapness and excellent service. The chic place to stay was the King David Hotel, later the target of a massive terrorist attack. Connoisseurs stayed at the American Colony. It had been founded by members of a religious sect from the American Midwest. They had come to Jerusalem in the 1920s to be on the spot in good time for the Second Coming, which according to their beliefs was scheduled I think for 1932. The Second Coming did not materialize, or at least not in any identifiable form, and these people had abandoned their homes and employment in the United States, and had no money for the return passage. Resourcefully, one group set up in the hotel business – hence the American Colony, which by the 1940s was the mecca of the discerning visitor to Jerusalem.

I have no idea how long we spent in Jerusalem, in that summer of 1942. We were also in Haifa, at Mount Carmel and at a small resort on the coast in the north called Nahariya. Here, perhaps, I glimpsed but in no way understood something of the ominous climate of the country and also of its loaded connection with Europe of the past and present. The *pension* at which we stayed – an unpretentious but attractive cluster of whitewashed buildings around a green lawn, with a vine-covered courtyard in which meals were served – was owned by Germans. I was instantly baffled and confused. German, to me, meant enemy. 'Please God, make the war end soon and may we win and not the Germans': my nightly prayer. But clearly there was nothing whatsoever that was hostile about these beaming people, who provided airy, spotless bedrooms, puddings drowning in cream, and who were evidently a part and parcel of the place. They had their own cows (furnishing all that cream, no doubt) and relatives just down the road who grew oranges and grapefruit. German? If anyone explained to me, the explanations washed over my head. I shrugged the problem aside, and concentrated on the important business of the beach facilities.

They must have been refugees of the 1930s. This must have been an area of German settlement – an early land purchase, in all probability. There they were, tending their cows and plying us with *apfelstrudel* and cream-topped milk-shakes. I can see still rooms with crisp gingham curtains, spanking white tablecloths and a pink-cheeked teenage girl who let me play with her kitten. In Nahariya I forgot my occasional nagging disquiet about what might be going on at Bulaq Dakhrur – were they remembering to feed the guinea-pigs? And would the Germans – those other Germans – treat our dog properly if they came? I settled down in Nahariya, and established my own emergency settlement, with its own absorbing daily concerns and occupations. There was a great sweep of sandy unpopulated beach beyond a belt of sand dunes. Lucy and my mother set up camp in the sand dunes, respectively knitting and sunbathing, and I patrolled the shore, searching for cowrie shells, of which I now had a seriously important collection. The high-water mark lay along the beach in a long curving frill and there, in the delicate surf of shell fragments, pebbles and fronds of seaweed, you could find, every now and then, tiny nacreous cowrie shells, pink and brown and white, perfect ovals, humped on one side and with neat serrated infolded edges on the other. It was like gathering pearls, and had all the appeal of the treasure-hunt: not too easy, but not so sparsely rewarded as to be frustrating. Obsession, once more. The absolute obsession of acquisitive greed. The other visitors said what a nice quiet industrious child I was.

And one night I was allowed to stay up after dark, for a treat and a surprise. We walked along the quiet roads of the settlement in the velvet warm night, and the place was on fire. Green fire. Every bush and tree shone with little emerald balls of light. Glow-worms.

I would have been happy to stay in Nahariya indefinitely. We moved on. My mother had got bored with lying among the sand dunes, and there was no social life. We went to Mount Carmel, where so far as I was concerned there was nothing of significance except that tree. And thence to Haifa, where I think we met other elements of the Cairo diaspora. There must surely have been perturbed discussion of the news from the Libyan front? If so, I was never aware of any undue anxiety. My father was still in Cairo, going daily to his office. Wondering, I would suppose, about us. What contingency arrangements had he made for his own departure, if things looked worse yet? I have no idea. The assumption was that all would be well, and in due course we would return to Egypt and life would go back to normal. As indeed was the case, but their optimism – or their unconcern – astonishes me, today.

In 1947 the British mandate came to an end and Palestine effectively ceased to exist. There would now be Israel, and the Palestinian problem. Foraging among those shards in my head, I try to find some signal that I knew the word Israel, and again all the connotations are biblical. Israelites – yes, indeed. I knew the term Jewish – we knew Jewish people in Cairo. I think I had a vague grasp of the concept of Judaism. I would have known that Christ was a Jew – the Bible said so. And the disturbing effect of the Church of the Holy Sepulchre had been perhaps the hazy perception that Christianity speaks in tongues. I would have known that expression, too, from the Bible, but it was the first time I had seen it in action, as it were. But I do not think that I had any understanding of anti-Semitism at the time, even in its most superficial social forms. Three years later, in London, my innocence came to an abrupt end. The first photographs from Belsen reached the English newspapers. My Harley Street grandmother, in whose care I then was, tried to keep them from me. Wrongly, I now think – twelve is old enough to be confronted with the nature of evil. But I can understand how she would have flinched. I came across the pictures, turning a page and glimpsing what appeared to be a grainy grey representation of piled dead people with matchstick limbs and skeletal faces. But this could not be so. I looked again, and saw that it was.

I grew up in a geographical area in which for a few years history had gone into overdrive. So much was happening so fast that even to read of it now is to be constantly checking dates and events, in disbelief at the fluidity of it all. Within a few years, the Germans had been poised to overrun Egypt and the rest of the Levant, but were halted. Allied and Axis forces ebbed and flowed across the desert, and then vanished entirely. In Egypt, the nationalist movement was quietly consolidating its position – there would not be much longer either for British rule or for King Farouk. And Palestine would soon cease to exist, translated into the distress and dissension of today. It is hardly surprising, I suppose, that a nine-year-old child should not take much of this on board. All the same, I look back with a certain wonder at that *alter ego*, collecting cowrie shells while the Middle East roared around her.

Chapter Eight

I had a more accurate perception of distance as a child than I have today. Now, like any other late-twentieth-century traveller, I believe that the Atlantic is as wide as it takes to read the newspaper and a few chapters of a book, eat a meal and have a snooze. I think that Australia is tiresomely inaccessible because it takes a whole twenty-four hours to get there, and if I were invited to lunch in Paris I might well accept. When last I went to Cairo, I was slightly put out because the journey did not quite give me time to finish a current reading chore and make some notes. The globe is diminished, reduced to time zones and unsettling climatic changes.

Once, I saw the world differently, and correctly. I knew that England was a very long way from Egypt, and that the two places were separated by tracts of sea across which you ploughed day after day, week after week, in a great ship that was itself a way of life. In fact, the voyage from Alexandria to Southampton by way of Gibraltar would have taken about a week, I think, but it was a week expanded by the excitement and exoticism of the process: in my recollection it was interminable. By the end, you knew that you had covered a great distance. Travel was a serious matter. We had trunks, labelled Not Wanted on Voyage, and special equipment by way of rugs and collapsible stools. My mother had hat boxes and something called a dressing case. My possessions, and Lucy's, went into a brown trunk with dark yellow ribs. It had to be searched for on docksides and station platforms: a symbol of security and normality. Later, it accompanied me for a few more years yet, to boarding school and even to university, with shreds of Bibby Line and P. & O. labels still clinging to it, hinting of another time and another world.

I knew that Palestine also was distant, though not nearly so distant as England, and understood that distance in terms of the Sinai desert, hour upon hour of it, and the obstacle of the Suez canal. Alexandria too was far off, but manageably far, a matter of hours, not days. Again, the distance was an actuality – that long road forging through the wastes of sand. I don't know when I learned to relate these known journeys to the map, and to see them in terms of global space, but when I did so I must have noted the great weight of Africa, hanging down there beneath the Mediterranean fringe of Egypt and Palestine.

In 1943, when my father was transferred to Khartoum, we did not move with him. My mother was reluctant to leave Cairo and it was considered that the Sudan climate was the ruin of European women and children. Men were thought to be made of sterner stuff, I suppose.

The idea was that we would join him there for the winter months, when the heat lets up a bit, and that he would take his leaves with us in Cairo or Alexandria. Thus, I plunged downwards into Africa for the first time.

The Sudan also was pink, of course, on the map. Or it may have been ambiguously pink, like Egypt – striped or dotted. The country was administered jointly by Britain and Egypt under the Condominion Agreement of 1899. There was a British Governor General and a Government House, as in Palestine. There was a Church of England cathedral and a bishop. My father, as an employee of an Egyptian bank, albeit a bank with strongly British connections, must have had a foot in both worlds. To me, Khartoum had plenty of superficial resemblances to Cairo, in the cultural sense, but was stiflingly hot, and unquestionably distant.

It was a distance that was again defiantly physical. The journey was a re-creation in tangible and vivid form of that dominant and significant winding black line on the map. We moved slowly down the Nile, from Cairo to Aswan and there we got on to a train which crawled on and down to Wadi Halfa and then across the neck of the Nile's great bulge to the left and then moved parallel with it again until at last we arrived at Khartoum. It took a long time. Ten days? About that, I should think, but, like those Mediterranean journeys, it became a separate unit of time, distinct from ordinary life, a capsule in which one was suspended in slow motion, trundling for ever down and down, into another place.

It was travel, as travel should be, and since I have never been back to Khartoum, I am left with one surviving correct impression of the relation between time and space.

It would have been possible to fly. There was a flying-boat service which plied between Cairo and Khartoum, and indeed further still down into the continent, but it was expensive and was used mainly by those on official business or in a hurry. We had time enough to spare. We negotiated the Nile as people had always done, and probably not a great deal faster. We boarded a Nile steamer and chugged slowly down through Upper Egypt, until we got to Aswan and the limits of the Nile's navigability in this type of craft. Ahead lay the cataracts, and the narrowing of the river.

I have done that journey since, in a tourist cruise boat. The steamer we took in 1943 was a passenger craft with three or four decks, as firmly hierarchical as the trains to Alexandria. There was the upper deck, which was first class and on which we rode. Individual cabins, dining and sitting saloons, a deck with awnings. Below was the second class, with sparser versions of these amenities, and below that yet was a pullulating free-for-all where people swarmed unconfined over open decks, cooking, sleeping, arguing. The boat hugged one bank, so that the other seemed so far away that you could barely see it. This was a wider, untamed Nile, not like the constrained and confined river which flowed through Cairo. And it went on, and on, and on. The steamer stopped frequently, for long periods. It would tie up for half a day at some riverside halt where people would pour on and off the lower deck and others proffered goods from the quayside: baskets of eggs, live chickens, oranges. Up in the higher regions, there was a certain amount of fretfulness. My mother muttered about the flying-boat. Lucy remarked that we might as well have walked, the time it was taking. And then at last we would be on the move again, after a great production over hoisting of gangways and casting off. I would settle down with my eyes glued to the muddy bank and the slopping shallows, waiting for crocodiles. So far as I was concerned, we were leaving the civilized world and heading into jungle country.

What I saw then – or did not see – is overlaid now by that subsequent visit, when I sat on the deck of a cruise boat and saw that incomparable Nile landscape with all the intrusions of adult understanding and experience. I saw how beautiful it is. Brilliantly coloured – emerald-green, ochre, feathered all over with the silver-blue of palms, splashed with the jewelled dots of figures in *galabiyas* of vermilion, salmon-pink, midnight-blue, *eau-de-Nil* (actually the *eau* of the Nile is a sort of greyish-buff). The soft light of the afternoon, with the desert hills beyond the cultivation pale buff and lilac, the palms throwing long quivering reflections on the water. Evening, the hills now pink and shedding a glow on to the river. The violent descent of night, when the sky turns a heavy peach colour and the river is suddenly blue, and within ten minutes it is quite dark. The birds: flocks of egrets like shredded white paper flying low over the water as the sun goes down, flights of brightly coloured ducks exactly like those in tomb wall paintings. A black ibis in silhouette on a spit of sand; a pelican patrolling the shore; a fish-eagle with golden head and shoulders perched on an overhanging branch. And the abiding interest of the river bank – clusters of mud huts like models of a prehistoric village, a man working a *shaduf*, women carrying water jars, children swinging from the huge leaves of a palm, and waving to the boat.

Back then, I must have seen all this, but differently. In the first place, I did not know that it was beautiful. It was profoundly familiar, and beauty to me would have implied something special and exotic. More significantly, I could not see it in terms of anything else. A perception of landscape is something learned – it depends upon individual knowledge and experience. At the age of ten, a mud hut to me was a mud hut, and could not be seen in the light of prehistory. A *shaduf* was a *shaduf*, and not a remarkable and ancient piece of engineering whereby water is raised from one level to another. Women carrying water jars were just that, without implications about health or economic circumstance. I probably noted the birds, but was far more interested in those potential crocodiles.

At Aswan we left the steamer and got on to a train to Wadi Halfa. There, it seems to me that we switched to a different train for the long haul across the loop of the

Nile and on down to Khartoum. Certainly, there is an impression of a great deal of waiting about on station platforms with all that that implied by way of crowds, commotion and aggravation. But I was used to this. I was a veteran of Egyptian trains and stations – Cairo, Alexandria, Ismailiya, Qantara, Suez – and knew what was normal. My mother and Lucy would have been in a fever about luggage and reservations and porters; I found the whole business distinctly stimulating. There was always a frenzied concourse of travellers of every gradation, insistent porters, obtuse officials, people begging and selling, droves of importunate children, stray dogs. The train would always be late, obstruction was rife, there would always be some drama about reservations not reserved or facilities not available. Each arrival or departure was a triumph over adversity. When in my adolescence I first saw the placid herds at English railway stations I was both perplexed and uneasy. Didn't these people understand that travel is a battle?

The train rocked across desert for what appeared to be days on end. About two, I now suspect, with a night in between. We had sleepers, an experience new to me and which I found entrancing. You woke in the cool dawn and there was the desert sliding past at the bottom of the bed, with the telegraph wires dipping up and down, up and down. There was nothing to see except an occasional camel train with Bedouin attendants, the animals festooned with equipment, the people shrouded so that they all seemed like moving parcels. The sand glittered with mirages, sometimes we moved through a great network of shining lakes and ribbed sand. This was Nubia, but I don't think I knew that at the time though it would have had a personal resonance. Daoud and Hassan, at Bulaq Dakhrur, came from Nubia, as did many domestic servants in Cairo, and I was well aware of their physical distinction from Abdul or Mansour – glistening night-black skin as against rich brown.

We reached Khartoum, and my father. I saw that this was indeed another country. Apart from anything else, it was hot. I was used to heat, but this was of another order. The heat imposed a curfew. You could not go out of doors between early morning and mid-afternoon. You rose early and walked by the river or in the zoo gardens for the bearable hours before the descent of that stifling pall. Then you languished all day in the muted heat of the stone-floored house, or on the shaded veranda, and sallied forth again as dusk fell. My father went to his office very early, and came home in the middle of the morning, going back to the office in late afternoon. We slept on the verandas of the house, on string beds without mattresses called *angareebs*. These were relished by the adults, for their relative coolness and – I suspect – the overtones of frontier life. I thought them primitive.

I remember those nights. The warm black velvet air, and then the raucous dawns, as the birds awoke. And before that there was the visit of the night-soil men who collected the latrine buckets – the pad of bare feet, the

tiny metallic clanks. I was much put out by this arrangement. In Cairo we had flush lavatories, for heaven's
sake.

We have been taken out sailing on the Nile by a friend
of my father's. This has been held up to me as a great
treat, but I am not enjoying myself at all. The sailing
boat is very small and I do not trust it an inch. One false
move and I shall be in there, helpless in the great
swollen green-brown flow of the water, with the crocodiles whipping up from below, jaws at the ready. My
parents know someone who is a close friend of a man
whose yacht capsized only last week and he swam for
the shore pursued by a crocodile and his strength gave
out only yards from safety. And he could do the crawl,
no doubt, I reflect grimly. I can only do breast-stroke.

I do not believe in these crocodiles. My impression
today is that even then there had not been crocodiles so
far down the Nile for many a year. It was a long time
since those Victorian and Edwardian drawings and photographs of *dahabiyas* cruising up-river with a line of dead
crocs slung from the bowsprit. I think they had long
since been shot out in that area and that my apprehension
was entirely atavistic. Fuelled no doubt by folklore and
anecdote. But there would be a certain satisfaction in
finding out that I am wrong, and that there was some
basis for that still potent anxiety.

We spent one winter only in Khartoum – two or

three months, perhaps — and what survives of it in my head is tenuous and oddly split into two opposing kinds of experience — one entirely sensuous and the other social and vaguely unnerving.

Khartoum was a sensuous place. That enveloping heat, as though you moved about swathed in warm cotton-wool. The lush and lurid gardens, in which all the plants were bigger and greener and more succulent than those at Bulaq Dakhrur. Trees and bushes with thick juicy leaves and flaming flowers in red and orange. The zoo, to which Lucy and I inevitably gravitated, was also a park in which many of the birds and animals roamed free. There were stately grey secretary birds which stalked up and down the paths; one once came up behind Lucy's back and tweaked her knitting needles out of her hand. Droves of little pig-like creatures rooted in the shrubberies. A baby elephant pottered about with its attendant keeper.

And then there were the Sudanese themselves, qualitatively different from Egyptians — plum-dark, smiling faces. Slower, jollier. I remember the heaped form of the watchman outside our gate, peaceably sleeping in the dust under a tree and leaping to attention at the sound of the front door opening. And the uniformed officials at my father's bank, with huge smiles and spanking white gloves and brass buttons. There is an impression of flowing voluminous white robes and those gleaming dark skins, an aspect of the sensuality of the place. Even the people seemed more vivid and intense.

All that was clear and precise, a question of observation and absorption. The other thing was on a different plane. It was perturbing, and somehow treacherous.

I joined the Khartoum Brownie pack. I had been a Brownie in Cairo, so this was not a new experience. Khartoum Brownies wore white uniforms instead of brown, with yellow ties, and Brownie gatherings took place in the grounds of the bishop's residence, implying in some way the blessing of the church. We did sing the occasional hymn, I think. Otherwise, we did the usual Brownie things. You could get badges for the acquisition of various skills – laying a table, doing up a parcel, sewing on a button, tying a reef knot. I aspired to badges and laboured assiduously at table-laying and so forth. I think I got some, in the end. But, far more importantly, I made a friend.

She had red hair. I cannot now remember her name, only the red hair, which impressed me. Something sparked between us. We were inseparable. We stood next to each other for inspection and when team-picking arose we picked each other. I looked forward avidly to the next Brownie afternoon. I recognize now an eerie affinity with the process of falling in love – that inescapable, inexorable obsession with another person.

I asked Lucy if this child could be invited to tea, at our house. Lucy's expression became strained. She did not reply. Later, she conferred with my mother. And later still it was conveyed to me – not explicitly but in some veiled way – that this would not do. Her parents were not, it seemed, the right sort of people. Yes, she was a nice little girl. But.

I digested this non-information. I felt rebuked and embarrassed, as though myself caught out in a solecism.

Why not rebellious? Affronted? I know now what it was all about. The child was from the other side of the tracks, socially speaking, in accordance with the complex but rigid structure of expatriate British life. Her parents ranked differently from mine, and the chasm was sufficient as to be unbridgeable except presumably on such neutral ground as the Brownie pack. An invitation to tea would have been a transgression of the rules. At the time, I did not understand at all, except to perceive that my own perception was lacking in some mysterious way. I even wondered if possibly my friend had some infectious illness. But I neither queried the dictum nor objected.

The experience was to be mirrored a few years later, in England, when in my adolescence I struck up a friendship with a boy my own age while staying with relatives, and again had it tacitly conveyed to me that I was short on social sensibility. Once more, I felt a sort of puzzled guilt, but touched this time with doubt, and years later was able to write a short story about the episode which has always served me as a neat illustration of the way in which reality furnishes fiction. But in Khartoum I accepted this denial of a relationship with regret but without resentment. Was I peculiarly docile? Lumpenly unquestioning? Or, as I would rather think, is this not an instance of the way in which a child simply assumes that adult codes must be correct? The task at that stage is not to query the codes, but to identify them. I had been caught out in a failure to identify, and felt accordingly humiliated. Later, at fourteen, I remember the interesting and disturbing tingle of query.

I have always been sceptical of the claim that travel broadens the mind. It depends how well equipped that particular mind was in the first place. Plenty of well-travelled minds are also nicely atrophied. Children are in any case of a different order. My own childhood exposure to the varying cultures of Egypt and – briefly – of Palestine and the Sudan left me with an awareness of differences, but not of differences that I could absorb in any meaningful way. I saw simply that there is no uniformity of persons nor of places. At nine, and ten, I was starting to look beyond the prison of my own concerns, but was still focused mainly on the physical world, as younger children are. And I was still, also, fettered by the abiding task of childhood – the penetration of adult assumptions. There is not much room for reflection about cultural differences when you are still doggedly trying to identify the requirements of your own immediate circumstances. When I try to recover those months in Khartoum, it is for the most part like trying to peer into a mist. There are dim shapes and impressions, and then here and there the sun pours down and something leaps into clarity. The sheen of those plum-dark skins, the brilliance of a flower. The sound of bare feet on a tiled floor. The strut of a secretary bird. Those atavistic lurking crocodiles. And the baffling system whereby one child could be invited to tea but another could not. And I think I understand now why it should be this curious miscellany that survives. It mirrors my own ten-year-old concerns – the dazzling appearance of the world, and the perversity of its ways.

Chapter Nine

Lucy and I left for England in a troopship. It was early spring – 1945. The troopship – the *Ranchi* – was *en route* from the Far East and India with a cargo of the armed forces bound for home and demobilization. She stopped off at Suez to pick up some more, and along with them a small consignment of women and children; 7,000 troops – 100 women and children. Can it really have been 7,000? That is the legendary figure that has lain in my head ever since. We never saw them. We boarded the ship and were immediately segregated in a civilian ghetto well out of the way of the licentious soldiery, presumably in the interests of our own well-being. I remember only crowded dormitories with bunk beds, and queuing for the bathroom with the two saltwater showers, and the sense of those hordes elsewhere. There was the stamp of boots overhead, and sometimes distant sounds of revelry. It was a far cry from the P. & O. and the Bibby Line. No deck chairs and solicitous stewards.

My mother was staying in Cairo with the man she was going to marry. My father would tie up his affairs in the Sudan and follow us to London in a few months. The war was not yet over, but the end was in sight. On the *Ranchi* everyone was elated – the invisible troops, the other expatriate women. Lucy was exuberant. Everyone was heading home, except for me, who was going into exile.

I was twelve, poised for adolescence, though a lot more child-like probably than any adolescent of today. I had little idea what lay ahead, but I knew that something had come to an end. I remember a feeling of sobriety, rather than of grief. I remember gazing theatrically at the spit of land at the mouth of the canal, as the ship headed for the open sea, and thinking that I was seeing the last of Egypt. I decided to keep a diary of this momentous journey, and began it by listing all the other ships we had seen berthed at Suez, along with further observations about military activities in the area. Lucy, a patriot to the core, became anxious about the implications of this, and mentioned the matter to the NCO supervising our ghetto, who said gravely that there might indeed be a security risk. Lucy told me to start again and stick to descriptions of our daily routine. This was not the sort of thing I had in mind at all, and I threw the diary away.

The journey is a blank, now – perhaps in consequence of that affront. I remember only incessant lifeboat drills on the deck, when everyone stood about and grumbled, and nights when we lay in our bunks hearing distant muffled thuds which were apparently depth charges. There were not supposed to be any German U-boats around in the Mediterranean but there was always the possibility, and when we turned into the Bay of Biscay and eventually up the Irish Channel the thuds became more frequent.

We were to dock at Glasgow. The ship entered the mouth of the Clyde, and the shoreline became visible. The 7,000 caught their first glimpse for several years of their native land and headed as one man for the port decks. There were frantic loudspeaker exhortations and after a few minutes the ship rode level once more. It was getting dark, anyway, a dank spring evening. By the time we tied up I was in my bunk, asleep.

I woke to an unnatural stillness, and monstrosity. Framed in the porthole was an immense hairy foot. A hairy hoof. I stared in disbelief, and rose to see my first Clydesdale horse, carrying out haulage duties on the quayside. It was pouring with rain, and bitterly cold. I knew that I had arrived in another world.

We took an overnight train to London, sitting up in a crammed compartment reeking of people in damp clothes, with Lucy on a high, pouring out our life histories to anyone who would listen, revelling in the camaraderie of her own language, her own country. I was acutely embarrassed, and pole-axed by the cold and what I could see out of the train windows, as it crept south in the grey dawn. The whole place was green, bright green. Grass, from end to end. How could this be?

I was dimly aware of the arrangements. I was to be

consigned to the care of my grandmothers – my paternal Harley Street grandmother in London and my maternal Somerset grandmother. My father would come to England as soon as he was able to. My mother would stay on at Bulaq Dakhrur with her new husband. I was going to boarding school. I knew all this, vaguely, and fended it off. For the moment, I had to come to terms with this stupefying environment: the inconceivable cold, the perpetually leaking sky, that grass.

My London grandmother met us off the train. I was almost as tall as she was now and did not remember her at all. Today, I can feel a wholehearted admiration for my grandmothers. They were both over seventy and had valiantly agreed to take on a twelve-year-old whom neither had set eyes on for six years. In their heads there must have been an engaging small child. What they now received was an anguished adolescent, for whom the world had fallen apart. For the next two years they shunted me from one to the other, with anxious instructions about clothing requirements and dental appointments.

They represented a classic English polarization – the town and country cultural divide. My Harley Street grandmother was the widow of a surgeon. She was still living in what had been both the family home and his consulting rooms – a five-floor house in that long sombre street. Today, there is an array of brass plates at the entrance of number 76. Back then, it was far from unusual for a single successful medical practitioner to occupy the entire house. My grandfather had died during the war, and my grandmother was now living like a squatter in her own home, entrenched within the old consulting room on the ground floor, which was the only room that could be kept warm. The rest of the building towered around her, the rooms shuttered and the furniture under dust-covers. Some of the windows had been blown out in the Blitz and never replaced – there were makeshift arrangements with boarding, and the occasional gaping hole.

Living there with my grandmother was a relative called Cousin Dorothy. She was elderly, in delicate health, stone deaf and distinctly unpleasant. She seemed to be the quintessential poor relation but also to have my grandmother dancing attendance on her. She spent her days in the most comfortable armchair, hogging the fire, swathed in shawls, and she used an ear trumpet. She took an instant dislike to me, correctly identifying a rival for my grandmother's attentions, and never referred to me except as 'the girl'. In the basement was Nellie the cook, governing her own subterranean territory which seemed to stretch away into infinity. The house was a classic example of the optimum-size early-nineteenth-century terrace mansion. It had all the accessories – an immense coal-hole under the pavement, a satellite cottage in the mews behind, sculleries and larders and a wine cellar and lowering kitchen ranges and a food-lift on a pulley that could be wound from top to bottom of the house. From my grandmother I learned the correct terminology for various sections, which is why I am one of the few people left to call the well between the basement of a London house and the pavement the area, and to know what the leads are (the open rooftop of a jutting extension at the back of the house – the sort of thing that would be made into a roof-garden these days).

There my grandmother had brought up six children, and there she now held out in a sort of gallant defiance of circumstances. She was a strong personality, a forceful woman with a robust sense of humour and artistic leanings. She was not a cosy grandmother, but a down-to-earth one, who set about what she no doubt saw as the rehabilitation of this waif washed up on her doorstep. No point in weeping and gnashing of teeth. The child must learn to adapt. I was plunged at once into the day-by-day negotiation with shortages and bureaucratic regulations which was the hallmark of the times. Each morning my grandmother sallied forth with a string bag in search of provisions. Offal was the supreme trophy. When she achieved this Holy Grail, she would plunge down into the basement calling for Nellie, and the two of them would pore in rapture over the bloody puddle of liver or kidneys. Lucy and I were officially non-persons, of course. The first task of all was to establish our existence and equip us with identity cards and ration books. Long hours in Marylebone Town Hall, waiting our turn to be quizzed by a hard-faced functionary. At last we achieved recognition. I had a blue ration book, as a person under sixteen. The functionary, thawing for an instant, pointed out portentously that I'd be entitled to bananas on that. My sense of disorientation was intensified. Why should people get excited about bananas?

My Somerset grandmother lived with my aunt Rachel in a place of red earth, steep lanes, flower-filled hedge banks, the long slack skylines of Exmoor and the slate-grey gleam of the Bristol Channel. She also was a widow, and at Golsoncott too life had been pared down, whittled away to a shadow of pre-war indulgence. But certain proprieties were observed. Dinner at eight, for which my grandmother changed from her day-time tweeds into a floor-length housecoat and her pearls. The time-honoured routine of church attendance, chairmanship of the village-hall committee and the Women's Institute, household shopping in Minehead on Tuesdays, a rigorous daily stint in the garden. To go there from Harley Street was to move from one cultural zone to another – even I could see that, with my fragile grasp of social niceties. The staccato scatter-shot of Cockney was replaced by the ruminative buzz of Somerset speech. In each place the other was looked upon with mistrust and contempt. In Somerset, everyone said I'd soon have some roses in my cheeks once I'd shaken off that smoky London air. In London they wondered what a child could possibly find to do down there. My Somerset grandmother visited London once a year. She called it 'going up to Town', and had special clothes which she wore on no other occasion. She would go to a theatre or concert, take lunch or tea with relatives, and retreat thankfully after three days to her rose garden and her embroidery. My Harley Street grandmother, for whom the wilderness began at Croydon, made a ritual trip to Kew Gardens in the spring and a quarterly day-return outing to see her sister in Staines, from which she would return complaining of the distance.

The journey to Somerset was itself a sort of acclimatization, from the moment you reached Paddington and the Great Western Railway train with its sternly regional black-and-white photographs of Glastonbury Tor and St Michael's Mount and Clovelly. At Taunton you crossed the frontier for real, changing into the branch line to Minehead. Norton Fitzwarren, Bishop's Lydeard, Crowcombe, Stogumber . . . The line is still there, but mockingly reborn as a 'scenic railway'. Back then, it wasn't scenery – it was a serious progress from A to B. People got on and off at every stop – schoolchildren, women returning from a day's shopping in Taunton, visiting relatives. Myself, alighting at Washford to be met by my grandmother in the old Rover with the running-board and medallion of St Christopher alongside the speedometer.

My Somerset grandmother was a strong personality also, but differently so. She too took me in hand, and was soon to do so alone after my Harley Street grandmother died. Her method was a kind of benign and tactful digestion of me within the calm parameters of her own concerns. She swept me up into a routine of brisk walks, local commitments, gardening chores and fireside evenings. She was the voice of authority, but she was also affectionate and companionable. She teased me when I began to strike adolescent attitudes, and punctured my burgeoning vanity. She came to say goodnight to me in bed every night, humming her way along the corridor. She could be both stern and indulgent. She had a youthful sense of the ridiculous. Once, the elastic in my knickers broke when we were out shopping in Minehead and they fell to the ground: we fled to the car and laughed ourselves into incoherence. And as I grew up, and became myself more opinionated, we frequently disagreed – energetically but without rancour. I came out as an agnostic, and went through the Ten Commandments with her to demonstrate that agnosticism was not synonymous with amorality – that I still held much the same views as she did on what was right and what was wrong. I queried her Conservatism – though I was not the first to do that. My aunt Rachel had always held somewhat socialist views which had been reinforced by her wartime experience working with an evacuee organization in East London.

In the fullness of time, Golsoncott became the approximation of a home, and my grandmother and aunt central to my life. But in those early months and years of exile I was still an alien, walking that landscape always with a faint sense of incredulity. Sooner or later, surely, I would wake up and find myself at Bulaq Dakhrur. This was all a mistake, and eventually it would be proven so and normality would be restored. Sometimes I felt as though I were in suspension, dumped here in this alien other world while somewhere else real life was still going on, golden and unreachable; at others I was swept by the grim apprehension that all this was true. It was really happening, and would continue to do so.

An enforced metamorphosis took place, during that spring and summer of 1945. I moved slowly from disbelief to resigned acceptance, and aged it seemed by about ten years. The war ended, and I hardly noticed, immersed in becoming someone else. At the most practical level, I had to be kitted out with a new wardrobe. Friends and relatives were called upon to sacrifice their clothing coupons. I must apparently have a tweed coat, and flannel skirts and thick jerseys. Knee-length socks, serge knickers, Chilprufe vests and a fearful woollen corset called a Liberty bodice. Lisle stockings and suspender belt, for heaven's sake. I . . . who had never in all my life worn anything other than a cotton frock. I protested. You're in England now, said Lucy grimly. She didn't need to remind me.

At some point during that first summer Lucy went away. I cannot now identify a moment of departure. She was there, for a while, and then she was not. And in the autumn I went to boarding school, to embark on the slow Calvary that was to last until I was sixteen.

Lucy moved on to spend many years with another family, where she received more consideration than I think she had from mine. I remained in contact with her until the end of her life. On one occasion when I was visiting her, not long before her death, she remarked suddenly that she had been having a clear-out and had come across some old letters of mine. Would I like to have them? I said I would. She couldn't remember right now where she'd put them, she said. She would send them.

In due course she did so. There were dozens of them, beginning that summer of 1945 and running on for the next few years. The later ones, when I was fifteen or sixteen, were unexceptional – long chatty accounts of what I had been doing. Grumbles about school. Adolescent posturing. Family gossip. It was the early ones that brought me up short, as I sat reading in my study through a long morning more than forty years later. They too were garrulous screeds about school, about the grandmothers, about what I had seen and done, but every now and then they broke down and became something else. They became love letters, and out of them there burst a raw anguish, a howl of abandonment and despair. I read them close to tears, incredulous, realizing that I remembered neither the writing of them nor the distress. It was possible to feel an acute and entirely detached pity. And when I had finished reading the letters I destroyed them all, because I knew that I could never bear to read them again, and because I knew also that I would not wish anyone else ever to do so. That sad child was gone, at rest, subsumed within the woman that I now am. And I think now of what it must have been like to be on the receiving end of those pathetic cries. Did she re-read them before she pushed them into that large manila envelope and posted them off to me? I think not. I suspect that she also, in her own way, had long since buried that traumatic separation.

The events and the impressions of those early months and years in what was allegedly my own country are compressed now into a medley of sensation, much of it physical. There was the cold, which was beyond anything I would have thought possible. In the famously hard winter of 1947 the snow came in through the blitzed windows at Harley Street and lay in unmelting drifts on the stairs. Staying with relatives somewhere in the country, I used to creep into bed with all my clothes on. At my boarding school on the south coast you had to break the ice on the dormitory water-jugs in the mornings before you could wash. I thought I would die of the cold: it would have been a merciful release.

This was England, then. But it bore no resemblance whatsoever to that hazy, glowing nirvana conjured up in the nostalgic chatter to which I had half listened back in Egypt. Back in the real world. Nobody had mentioned the cold. Or the rain. Or the London dirt which was not the aromatic organic dirt of Egypt but a sullen pervasive grime which left your hands forever grey and every surface smeared with soot. In my mind I had created a place which seems like those now out-dated advertisements for environmentally destructive products like petrol or cigarettes – all soft-focus landscape, immutable good weather, gambolling animals and happy laughing folk. I had never seen such advertisements and I suspect the image was based on Mabel Lucie Attwell illustrations spiced with Arthur Rackham and Beatrix Potter. Certainly I would not have been surprised to find toadstool houses and the odd gnome, or people wearing poke bonnets and pinnies. I might well have felt on home ground then – I had grown up with that kind of thing, in a sense.

What I was confronted with was something that was in no way soft-focus but disconcertingly precise. The weather was precise and inescapable, the topography was precise and daunting, what was expected of me was precise but coded. The gambolling animals had been turned into offal, and the happy laughing folk were transformed into the po-faced raincoated ranks at bus stops or on railway platforms. Moreover, everyone else knew their way around. They had the maps and the passwords. They did not so much exude happiness or laughter as an implacable confidence. This was their place. They had wrapped it round them and pulled up the drawbridge.

I believe I have some idea of how the refugee feels, or the immigrant. Once, I was thus, or nearly so. I had concerned relatives, of course, and I spoke the language but I know what it is like to be on the outside, to be the one who cannot quite interpret what is going on, who is forever tripping over their own ignorance or misinterpretation. And all the while I carried around inside me an elsewhere, a place of which I could not speak because no one would know what I was talking about. I was a displaced person, of a kind, in the jargon of the day. And displaced persons are displaced not just in space but in time; they have been cut off from their own pasts. My ordeal was a pale shadow of the grimmer manifestations of this experience, but I have heard and read of these ever since with a heightened sense of what is implied. If you cannot revisit your own origins – reach out and touch them from time to time – you are for ever in some crucial sense untethered.

I was used to a society in which people were instantly recognizable, defined by dress and appearance. An Egyptian could easily enough be distinguished from a European; someone who was English was unlike someone who was Greek. And the same was true here in England, it seemed, except that I could not see it. They all looked much the same to me, the raincoated London throngs. I could hear differences of speech, but these were confusing rather than illuminating. And the subtle code of appearance was quite beyond me. There were sartorial requirements which applied to me also, it seemed. You must never go out without gloves and an umbrella. Well, the umbrella made sense – but the gloves were purely symbolic, so far as I could see. They indicated what sort of person you were. They indicated what sort of a home you came from and quite possibly vouched for your character as well, for all I knew. 'Where are your gloves?' my grandmother would inquire on the

Harley Street doorstep, kindly but sternly. And back inside I would have to go, to equip myself with my credentials before we could set forth.

And then there was the matter of the divorce. My parents had not split up, in the brisk and neutral phraseology of today – they were divorced, a word that reeked of taboo. I soon learned that the situation should not be mentioned, or at least only by adult relatives in an awkward undertone. At my boarding school there was a small handful only of other girls with divorced parents. The headmistress summoned me to a private interview and made it clear that my position was unfortunate but distinctly reprehensible, and the most expedient behaviour was to lie low about it.

I tried to hitch myself to this place in the most basic way. I tried to find my way around it. In Somerset I pottered in the lanes and fields, contentedly enough. In London I roamed about, alone for the most part. Sometimes my grandmother took me on excursions, and succeeded in transmitting to me something of her own partisan enthusiasm for the city she had lived in all her life. But she encouraged me also to take off on my own – sensibly enough, though this now seems a surprising indulgence. Perhaps London was a safer place for a loose teenager in those days than it is now. I rode buses hither and thither, collecting those differently coloured tickets – rose, lilac, buff, sixpence, ninepence, one and six – and learning how the place fitted together.

It was a landscape still scarred and pock-marked by

the Blitz. Houses leered from boarded windows, or simply yawned with cavernous black rectangles. They dripped plaster and sprouted greenery. Paving stones would give way to a sudden wasteland of dirt and rubble. Railings were replaced by planks and lengths of rope. There were sudden eloquent gaps. A space in a terrace of houses where you would see ghostly staircases running up exposed walls, or a spine of cast-iron fireplaces with mantelpieces, and the unexpected intimacy of floral wallpaper. Or a sudden plunging hole filled with rubble and the jungle growth of bramble and buddleia that had swarmed into the vacuum.

It seems now a long way from the London of today – a slow, scruffy dirty place in which the traffic crept along sedately and you woke in the mornings to the sound of hoofs, the leisurely clop of the United Dairies pony, delivering the milk. Coal was shot down under the pavements – a sackful at a time – black treasure measured out into the grate lump by lump. At Harley Street there was the one fire in the consulting room, monopolized by Cousin Dorothy, and elsewhere frigid expanses, as cold as out of doors. Little hissing gas fires in the bedrooms, those brittle grey columns in front of which you could get your legs nicely scorched if you sat close enough. I would retreat to mine and find solace in a bar of Fry's chocolate and a book from the dust-covered glass-fronted bookcases in the drawing-room. My grandmother was a devotee of Charlotte M. Yonge. I read *The Daisy Chain* and *The Heir of Redclyffe* from end to end, to oblige, with my knees scarlet and the back of me shivering. And Harrison Ainsworth and G. F. Henty and John Buchan, more fodder from the shelves in this new world where even the fiction was otherwise. No Arthur Ransome at Harley Street, and if there was any Greek mythology I never found it.

Friends and relations rallied round. There were theatre visits, lunches and teas. I was posted off for weekend visits, clutching my railway ticket, correctly gloved, with my umbrella strapped to my suitcase. I must have been a dismaying guest – incongruously tall, like a bolted lettuce, socially inept, crippled by homesickness.

I no longer know which of these family friends it was who hit on the idea of taking me to see the heart of the City, the bomb-flattened area around St Paul's. He was someone who had developed an intense interest in the topographical history of the area and had discovered the way in which the bombs had stripped away the layers of time. He had taken to going down there, map in hand, to trace what was revealed. He suggested I come with him on one of these weekend excursions.

The place was deserted. St Paul's rose from a waste-land of rubble, cropped walls and sunken lakes of willow-herb. The effect was not one of destruction but of tranquil decay, like some ruined site of antiquity. Street signs tacked to surviving shreds of wall plotted the layout of the place: Cheapside, Bread Street, Watling Street. We wandered around, peering down into the pink flowered lakes (DANGER! KEEP OUT!), inspecting the untidy little cliffs of walling, matching what we saw against my companion's street plan of the pre-war City. He also had a plan of the medieval boundary wall. He showed me how this was reflected in the street pattern. He gave me a genial history lesson, most of which I could not follow because what I knew of English history was confined to the patriotic rantings of *Our Island Story*, but I paid attention. I became distinctly interested. I floated free of the prison of my own discontents and enjoyed the fresh air of an abstract interest. I caught a glimpse of what it is like to have adult concerns. Look, said my companion, here is a stretch of the actual medieval wall, which must have been embedded within and beneath this blitzed building – look at the flint and ragstone. And then he led me to his *pièce de résistance*. Here, he said with triumph, here is a Roman bastion. This was one of the corners of the oldest wall of all, the original Roman wall.

Roman? *Roman*, had he said? But what did this mean? We had Romans down in Egypt. Had had Romans, time was. I knew about Romans. They came from Rome and Italy and surged all over Egypt and Palestine, building forts and temples and things which had fallen down but bits of which you could still see. They dropped their money everywhere: most of it was in Alexandria Museum. They built the Alexandria catacombs. They were responsible for Pontius Pilate. So how then could there be Romans right up here, in England?

I pondered this, staring at that unexceptional bit of

wall. Evidently *Our Island Story*, in its potted hagiography of Boadicea, had not made it clear who it was she was up against. Perhaps I asked my companion to explain matters. If so, I don't remember. What I do remember, with a clarity that is still exhilarating, is the sudden sense of relevances and connections which were mysterious, intriguing and could perhaps be exposed. That word Roman chimed a note that was personal but was also, I realized, quite detached. Romans were to do with me because I had heard of them, but they were also to do with the significant and hitherto impenetrable mystique of grown-up preoccupations. It was as though the exposure of that chunk of wall had also shown up concealed possibilities. I sniffed the liberations of maturity, and grew up a little more, there amid the wreckage of London and the seething spires of willowherb.